ADVANCE PRAISE OF
Small Town Rage: Fighting Back in the Deep South

"David Hylan preserves the voices of those who refused to be silent when silence was killing us. *Small Town Rage* honors the courage of a community abandoned by its leaders, churches, and neighbors yet determined to demand humanity in the Deep South. This book reminds the world that activism didn't just happen in coastal cities; it took root in Shreveport, in the Bible Belt, where speaking out came with a price. ACT UP Shreveport was more than a movement—it was a lifeline. Our rage was small only in geography. In heart and purpose, it was boundless."

—ACT UP Shreveport

"David Hylan has written a powerful book on HIV in the South—in Louisiana—at the beginning of the epidemic when the only response had to be one of rage, solidarity, love, rebellion and advocacy in the form of ACT UP-Shreveport. A beautiful tale of hope and ultimate transcendence in the fight against AIDS in the deep South."

—Monica Gandhi, MD Director,
UCSF-Bay Area Center for AIDS Research (CFAR)

"David Hylan's beautiful prose is in stark contrast to the apathy, ignorance, and outright persecution that he documents in this jolt to the conscience of a city that equated conformity with character and homosexuality with eternal damnation. Hylan's writing deeply honors the desperate struggle of local AIDS activists as they realized the fight couldn't be limited to the highly publicized coastal cities, but that 'ordinary people refusing to wait quietly for permission to live' could act up anywhere! And did they ever: opening eyes, saving lives, building a strong community, bringing lasting change, and paving the way for future activists in this deeply conservative Southern city."

—Adrienne Critcher, PhD, Co-Founder of PACE,
People Acting for Change and Equality, NW Louisiana's primary
advocacy organization for the LGBTQ+ community

"From protest lines to hospital halls, ACT UP Shreveport fought for one thing above all—dignity. David Hylan's *Small Town Rage* honors that fight, reminding us that The Philadelphia Center stands as its living legacy."

—Chris Miciotto, LCSW-BACS, ACSW,
Executive Director, The Philadelphia Center

SMALL TOWN RAGE
Fighting Back in the Deep South

Dr. David W. Hylan

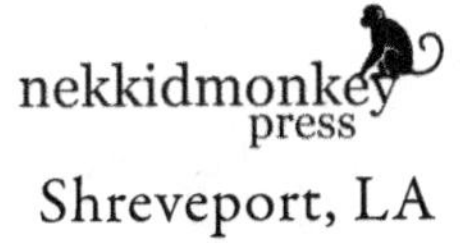

nekkidmonkey press
Shreveport, LA

nekkidmonkey press
413 Sleepy Hollow Rd
Shreveport, LA 71115
nekkidmonkeypress@gmail.com

This paper is acid-free and meets all ANSI standards for archival quality paper.

Printed in the United States of America

For my husband, Troy—my anchor.
For my children, Kristi, David, and Ashley—my light.
Thank you for believing in every dream,
and for lifting me when I stumbled.

NOTE

The documentary film *Small Town Rage: Fighting Back in the Deep South* (2016), co-directed by Dr. David W. Hylan and Raydra Hall, is available for public viewing on YouTube.

https://youtu.be/uDSv_p2XBnY

TABLE OF CONTENTS

FOREWORD
by Mark S. King

I couldn't wait to escape Shreveport.

The morning after my high school graduation ceremony in 1978, I loaded up the rusty Plymouth my parents had given me and I headed south to the fabled Big Easy, where my first year of college would begin at the University of New Orleans.

Never mind that it would be months before classes began. I had taken flight, away from small town prejudices and its blatant homophobia, and away from a family that had endured—with as much love as a brimming impatience—the embarrassment of a gay son who refused to hide himself. My parents hadn't questioned my quick exit. They helped me load my bags, kissed me in the driveway and waved goodbye.

What I was accelerating towards was the bigger life I thought I deserved, in a community that would accept—even embrace—what so much of Shreveport viewed as abhorrent.

It was a choice that came to haunt me as the years passed.

After college I made my way to even greater gay pastures, relocating to West Hollywood, California. I had found my tribe, the chosen family you hear about when queer people create familial intimacies. I had friends and lovers and a life that I built from scratch, even as my calls home to Shreveport occurred less often. Thousands of miles away, nieces and nephews were being born, and with it, babies I couldn't hold and names of new relatives I couldn't remember.

I had chosen gay community over family and the town I had fled—and that was fine by me.

Then the plague arrived.

Within a few horrific years, West Hollywood, the very place in which I had sought safety, became an epicenter of the murderous AIDS pandemic. It was no longer a city of dreams, but nightmares. My once thriving neighborhood became a tomb.

Then, in March of 1985, only weeks after the first HIV antibody test became publicly available, I tested HIV positive. There were no medications, no resources, and few options for support.

I threw myself into the HIV arena, finding a job at the first AIDS organization established in Los Angeles, LA Shanti. We trained volunteers on our model of compassionate presence, preparing them to provide comfort for the dying.

The horror of daily life in West Hollywood was beyond comprehension—much less explanation—so I withdrew further from my family back home. I didn't want them to worry, but the truth may be that I didn't want them to be ashamed. How could anyone in Shreveport, Louisiana possibly understand?

The answer to that question is within the pages of this book, David Hylan's exhaustive account of how ACT UP Shreveport transformed the care for, and awareness about, people living with and affected by HIV/AIDS in one southern city.

Chuck Selber, Gary Cathey, and Joe DeSantis arranged to meet at a diner one evening in Shreveport, and together they birthed a resistance. While I kept my distance from Shreveport and all it represented, these three men—like the many, many men and women their work would come to include—returned to Shreveport from lives elsewhere, from bigger places like Houston and New York City, and walked back into a lion's den of ignorance and rejection. They were joined by similarly courageous people who had never left in the first place. Together, they faced head-on what I had once feared the most.

ACT UP Shreveport redefined a city. And in doing so, they redefined my own life. Now, when I return home to visit the extended family that fate has allowed me to come to know, I no longer view Shreveport with the mixture of regret and disdain I once did.

ACT UP made Shreveport a city of heroes, a city of enlightenment, and a city that can be bent to the will of honorable people. The incredible true story you are about to read explains exactly how that happened.

In the years following my diagnosis, I carved a place in HIV activism as an outspoken writer who chronicles what we experienced, collectively and individually, and its reverberations across the decades. Maybe that's why I was asked to write this foreword, which is a tremendous honor.

But let's be clear. The men and women of ACT UP Shreveport did something gutsier than I ever have.

They stayed, or they returned home. And, against intimidating odds, they made it better.

(Mark S. King is a GLAAD Award-winning writer and the author of *My Fabulous Disease: Chronicles of a Gay Survivor*.)

PREFACE

The first time we sat down to film, I thought I understood what we were asking.

I didn't.

The camera changed the room. It asked for truth in a way conversation never had. For some, it opened a door. Stories came quickly—years of silence breaking all at once. For others, it was something harder. The weight of it settled before a single word was spoken. You could feel it in the pauses, in the way people held themselves, in what they chose not to say.

The interviews were never neutral. They were invitation and exposure at the same time.

People cried. Sometimes quietly, as if they were trying not to disturb something already broken. Sometimes without warning, as memory pushed past whatever had kept it contained for years. Others laughed—sharp, unexpected bursts at the audacity of what they had lived through, what they had dared to do. And sometimes they spoke in a steadier voice, carrying the quiet weight of survival.

When the film was finished, I believed we had done something complete. Ninety-eight minutes that carried voices, history, and a kind of reckoning.

It was not enough.

Stories remained. Not because they were less important, but because time has limits and film has edges. What didn't fit stayed with me—conversations that continued after the camera stopped, details that deepened rather than closed the story.

This book began there.

Not as an expansion, but as a return. A way to sit longer. To follow what the film could only touch. To give space where there had only been fragments.

Time changed my understanding of what we had captured. These voices were not just documentation. They were instruction. They were warning. They were unfinished.

This book is an attempt to carry what the film could not contain.

— Dr. David W. Hylan

INTRODUCTION

The people in this book never dreamed their names would be bound to a plague. In the early 1980s, they were never meant to be remembered at all. Yet the crisis pulled them into the pages of history.

They didn't march down Broadway or storm Capitol Hill. They didn't have the spotlight, the budget, or the luxury of being fashionable in their fury. They lived and raged in Shreveport, Louisiana—a city caught between contradictions, where Bible verses were painted on billboards and whispered at deathbeds, where AIDS arrived with shame, silence, and a sentence.

This is the story of ordinary people—mostly gay men and the friends who loved them—who chose not to disappear. Told to sit down, shut up, repent, or die, they instead stood up, made noise, demanded care, and insisted on dignity.

It is born from the documentary film *Small Town Rage: Fighting Back in the Deep South* (2016), produced and directed by David Hylan and Raydra Hall, but it is not the film retold. I was there for that telling, but this project asks more. The film captured what it could in ninety-eight minutes, but grief does not fit neatly inside a limited runtime. This book opens wider. It breathes. It lingers. It walks with the people behind the placards and chants. It lets us sit beside them at hospital beds, hear the quiet as much as the clamor, and feel the weight of what it meant to be queer, sick, furious, and alive in a place like Shreveport, Louisiana.

This is a Southern story—but not the kind pressed onto postcards. It's the South of sweat and struggle, where resistance was dug from red clay and stitched through scripture. It's about people who dared to believe their voices mattered, even when the halls of power, exam rooms, pulpits, and porches all tried to silence them.

It started as a whisper at the beginning of the epidemic, when doctors in coastal cities began noticing a strange pneumonia and a rare cancer killing gay men. The first known cases surfaced in New York and Los Angeles. A few doctors raised alarms. A few articles appeared. But no one listened.

Some say it began in Africa. Others trace it to a flight attendant from Canada—Gaëtan Dugas, a man the press hastily branded "Patient Zero," as if one person could carry the weight of a global catastrophe. It made for an easy headline and an easier scapegoat. The truth was more complicated than a single name. The virus didn't need a villain to spread. It needed silence. In those early years of the epidemic, silence was everywhere.

DeDe DeSantis McClamroch, sister of Joe DeSantis, a founding member of ACT UP Shreveport, later reflected: "I am reminded of dark days when the struggle was real. Death was on America's doorstep with so much fear. Judgment was rampant, and nothing was being done to help. We did not have any real help or support."

By the mid-1980s, what mattered wasn't just that the virus spread, but how slowly anyone cared—including in Shreveport, Louisiana, where even churches that preached Jesus' command to feed the hungry and care for the sick found ways to look away. By the time rumors reached our corner of the Deep South, the epidemic had already carved deep wounds into distant cities. We heard about New York, San Francisco, and Los Angeles. Here, it was easier to believe the threat was distant—an "elsewhere" disease. That false comfort bought time to look away, and time was exactly what the virus needed to slip in unnoticed.

In the early years, it was only rumors. Friends "losing weight." Someone "not looking well." Illness without a name, or with names no one wanted to say out loud. Rumors of a "gay cancer" clung to the air like humidity, heavy and hard to breathe. On the coasts, the fear already had a name. Here in Shreveport, it was static—until it wasn't. Friends in our community grew thin, got sick, and were gone, as Deborah Allen, an early ACT UP Shreveport member, would later say: "Our friends were passing away. They'd get very thin, and the next thing we heard, they had died. That's when we realized AIDS had come to Shreveport."

In a city where few dared to admit they even knew a gay person—let alone were one—the virus was treated like a rumor you could wish away. In Shreveport, Louisiana, during the early years of the AIDS epidemic, it didn't make it into church bulletins or city council meetings. It slipped between the cracks, unwelcome and unnamed. The response wasn't ignorance—it was performance: prayers instead of policy, sympathy instead of services. Churches thundered with brimstone. Doctors leaned back—quiet, cautious, complicit. Gay men became persona non grata—unwelcome everywhere. Politicians filled their calendars with anything else. And the local media? They simply turned the page.

This was the environment into which ACT UP Shreveport was born in the late 1980s. Across the country, larger cities were already mobilizing. In New York, playwright and activist Larry Kramer—whose fury helped spark a national movement—stood before a packed room in 1987 and demanded action, helping ignite what would become ACT UP. The movement became known for being confrontational, creative, united, and uncompromising, refusing to wait for permission to survive.

Years later, in 1991, Kramer stood before another audience, his anger sharpened by loss and inaction, and shouted what others still refused to say: "Plague! We are in the middle of a fucking plague. And you behave like this. Plague! 40 million infected people is a fucking plague! We are in the worst shape we have ever, ever, ever been in. All those pills we're shoveling down our throats, forget it." Larry Kramer called apathy a form of complicity.

As ACT UP Shreveport member Cecil Thad Coburn, one of the group's most reflective strategists, later put it, "For me, it took a while to see the true purpose of ACT UP and activism—to be 'sand in the gears' of a machine that's trying to grind you up, whether intentionally or not."

And yet, in Shreveport, the urgency felt far away—until it hit home. By the late 1980s, funerals became more frequent. Names slipped from address books to memorial lists. The faces on the coasts could just as easily have been the ones at our dinners, our barbecues, our Mardi Gras krewes. Slowly, it became clear that the same rage fueling protests in New York and San Francisco had found a place here. One of the first to articulate it was Chuck Selber—an outspoken Jewish activist, playwright, and one of ACT UP Shreveport's earliest and fiercest voices—who insisted, "Silence equals death. We had to shock them. We had to make them see what they refused to see." That insistence wasn't abstract. It was personal, local and timely, and it would have to force its way through walls of conservatism, racism, religious judgment, and willful neglect that had stood in this region for generations.

At the time, in the late 1980s, I was still in the closet—watching from the edges, pretending I had no stake in the fight while every death felt like it was chiseling my own name into a headstone. I was not among them in the streets. I was not carrying banners or shouting through a bullhorn. But I was there in another way—absorbing it, feeling it, understanding exactly what was at stake while telling myself I could remain separate from it.

I agreed with every word shouted into the air and felt the same white-hot anger at the cruelty, the neglect, the endless funerals. I was exhausted—bone-deep, soul-deep—from pretending, from biting my tongue, from holding my breath in a city that would have cheered to see us disappear.

This is how it happened—how a small, unlikely group of people in Northwest Louisiana decided they would no longer sit quietly while they and their friends died. How they staged protests, crashed meetings, and made themselves impossible to ignore. How they fought not just for survival, but for dignity in a place where neither was guaranteed—and where asking for either could cost you everything.

This book does not shy away from rage. It honors it. It names it. And it traces what that rage became: a movement, a memory, and—most of all—a legacy that took shape in Shreveport.

They never imagined their lives would carry that weight. Yet history made it so.

Several of them were supposed to die quietly.

Some did.

Others didn't.

The ones who lived carried more than the virus. They carried empty chairs at dinner tables, birthdays missed, phone calls that never came. They carried the sound of machines in hospital rooms that fell silent too soon, the smell of flowers wilting on headstones, the ache of holding someone's hand and knowing it was for the last time. They bore guilt for surviving when others didn't. They carried anger that survival had to be fought for—and a deeper anger that survival had to be fought for at all. And yet, even with grief stitched into every step, they kept moving into the years that followed.

They fought.
Fought to live.
Fought to be seen.
Fought to be heard.
They fought grief.
They fought silence.
They fought shame.
They fought the government.
They fought the hospitals.
They fought the church.
They fought their neighbors.
And some fought their families.

They fought for each other—in hospital rooms where curtains stayed closed, in courtrooms where justice was rationed, and in the streets of Shreveport, where their presence alone was defiance. In Shreveport, you weren't just fighting AIDS. You were fighting racism baked into politics, religion twisted into judgment, and a city that preferred to look away.

They fought back.

This is the story of fighting back in a small town in the Deep South. It begins in Shreveport—a place of contradictions, where churches thundered louder than hospitals, where scripture traveled faster than medicine, and where silence became a weapon during the worst years of the epidemic.

This is the story of ACT UP Shreveport.

I knew many of the people who were part of this journey. They were more than names, more than fragments of a story told too quickly and too late. They deserved to be seen fully, to be remembered as they lived—not only in protest, but in the quiet moments between, in the lives they built and the ones they lost. They deserved someone to say: I see you. I hear you. I understand what this cost. This book is my way of honoring them—of carrying forward what could not be contained and refusing to let it be forgotten. This is what I owe them.

The story does not begin with protest. It does not begin with a march, or a meeting, or even a name. It begins with a place—with its contradictions, its silences, its unspoken rules about who belonged and who did not.

To understand what happened here, you have to understand where it happened. You have to begin with a WELCOME TO SHREVEPORT.

CHAPTER 1
WELCOME TO SHREVEPORT

"They have no place in our society ... As God says in his Word, their penalty is death, which is proven true with the advent of AIDS."
—Dorothy B. Wynn, Letter to the Editor, *The Shreveport Times*

Silence nearly erased a city's dead. In the early 1980s, as AIDS crept into Shreveport, it settled like August heat—clinging to the skin, until it left a mark. They called it a plague. But no alarms sounded. No press briefings. No church vigils. No front-page headlines. The President stayed quiet. Churches looked away. Newspapers turned pages. Conversations dropped when certain names came up. Doctors avoided eye contact. Funeral homes turned families away, refusing services and shaming the dying like lepers at the gate. Even within the community, stillness rooted itself—born of fear, shame, and the hope that if no one spoke the words aloud, it might not be true.

At first, the country called it the "gay cancer"—an easy label for something they refused to understand. But as deaths mounted and the pattern became undeniable, the terminology shifted: Gay-Related Immune Deficiency, or GRID, then Acquired Immune Deficiency Syndrome—AIDS. Caused by HIV, it dismantles the immune system piece by piece until the body's defenses collapse. Pneumonia, cancers, meningitis—an avalanche of opportunistic illnesses. People weren't dying from one cause—they were dying from many at once. And the disease didn't just ravage the body—it exposed a moral fracture in a conservative, Christian city's conscience.

Louisiana had its own music—gospel wail, zydeco stomp, brass-band swagger—but Shreveport carried a different cadence, shaped by the long shadow of East Texas just down the road. This was not New Orleans exuberance or Acadiana intimacy. It was a border-city restraint, where conservatism traveled easily across state lines and settled in place, while religion functioned less as refuge than as regulation. Courtesy mattered. Appearances mattered. Silence was often mistaken for civility, and civility for virtue. In such a place, difference was not confronted; it was managed quietly—and when crisis came, that instinct shaped everything that followed.

Long before a virus tested its mercy, Shreveport had already shown what happened when its order was challenged.

In 1963, Shreveport's police commissioner, George D'Artois— already notorious for his brutality, a local counterpart to Birmingham's Bull Connor—rode a horse into Little Union Baptist Church on Milam Street in Shreveport during a memorial for the four Black girls murdered in the Birmingham church bombing. He dragged Reverend Harry Blake from the pulpit and had him beaten so badly that Blake required stitches.

The next day, eighteen students protesting the attack were arrested. One of them, Calvin Austin—a teenager from Shreveport—spent forty-five days in jail and was banned from every public school in Caddo Parish. He finished high school in New Orleans, a reminder that survival carried a cost for anyone outside the city's white, Protestant power structure. This wasn't distant history. The same churches, the same officials, and the same unwritten rules were still in place when AIDS arrived.

As one Black Shreveporter recalled—speaking only on the condition of anonymity—"If you were Black in Shreveport, you already knew the rules. You learned early what you couldn't say, where you couldn't go, and who you couldn't trust." To be Black meant knowing your place. To be queer meant hiding. To be sick meant disappearing. Respectability was currency. And for those living with HIV or AIDS, the message was unmistakable: don't get sick, don't speak up, don't expect help.

Shreveport was a city weathered by judgment and polished by generations of denial. It dressed tradition in its Sunday best—polished on the surface, unyielding beneath. Church wasn't optional—it was cultural law. Even silence had manners.

Antebellum homes and oil-money mansions stood as monuments to inheritance, their columns polished and hedges trimmed, power preserved in wrought iron and wealth. Behind those gates, generations of influence—built on gas fields and courthouse handshakes—watched the world shift and quietly prayed it wouldn't.

Some of those handshakes happened in the open at Freeman and Harris Café. By the time the AIDS crisis reached Shreveport, Freeman and Harris had become a pillar of the city's African American community—and a quiet crossroads where familiarity, discretion, and power intersected. Plates moved steadily from kitchen to table beneath the low murmur of a dining room that had seen generations pass through. Tucked in a majority-Black neighborhood, the café was one of the rare places where Black and white patrons shared tables, even in the strictest years of segregation.

But what happened at Freeman and Harris went far beyond food or history. It was a political crucible, where power dressed casually and promises were shaped over coffee cups—racial lines blurring just long enough to secure another term.

During the years when AIDS was tightening its grip on Shreveport, some of the same men who lingered over plates of stuffed shrimp and exchanged good old boy backslaps also controlled hospital budgets, public-health priorities, and whether help ever reached the people who were dying. Those decisions rippled far beyond the worn wooden floors of Freeman and Harris Café.

Shreveport's power elite weren't loud; they didn't need volume to dominate. They smiled for church directories, clinked glasses at charity balls, and drew their boundaries in invisible ink—lines you only discovered after crossing them. Each spring, they gathered beneath chandeliers for the Holiday in Dixie Cotillion, a ritual of lineage where sons and daughters of wealth were presented like heirlooms. Tens of thousands of dollars flowed for gowns and orchestras, yet none of that generosity reached those wasting away across town with HIV or AIDS. And whenever disturbance came—whether a march for Black rights, a visible queer life, or a disease that arrived without shame—their answer was always the same: contain it, not heal it.

Religion didn't just echo from pulpits in Shreveport; it governed from them. Sunday sermons bled into Monday meetings. Sanctuaries became

     DR. DAVID W. HYLAN

staging grounds for policy, and scripture was wielded like ordinance. When AIDS appeared, the first response wasn't medicine—it was moral judgment. Homosexuality wasn't framed as difference; it was branded as sin.

In that climate, many queer people in Shreveport learned early to measure their words and their lives. Religion was not just belief; it was enforcement. Sermons supplied the explanation long before doctors offered answers. Fear did the rest.

It wasn't only sermons that framed AIDS as punishment. Letters printed in the city's paper of record turned private judgment into public declaration. Citizens wrote that gay men had no place in society, that AIDS proved God's will, that suffering was the consequence of breaking divine rules. Some warned that homosexuality threatened the future of humanity itself. Others insisted that people deserved the pain they brought upon themselves. The language varied, but the message did not: illness was not a crisis to be met—it was a verdict already rendered.

Prejudice and callousness curled through the city like smoke—visible, inhaled, but rarely named.

For white, straight, middle-class residents, life kept a steady beat: Sunday chicken dinner, Monday-night visitation calls, Wednesday Bible study, Thursday choir rehearsal, Friday night football. The week moved in a loop of fellowship halls and padded pews. But beneath that ordered surface, the city strained.

There was a hum in the walls, a pressure in the air—things everyone felt but no one said out loud. Racism. Poverty. Addiction. Homophobia. And now, a virus with no name moving quietly from body to body. Shreveport wasn't merely uninformed; it was willfully blind.

By the early 1980s, rumor hardened into fact. Friends were vanishing—first the weight, then the laughter, then the names no one said out loud anymore. A strange illness in New York, then San Francisco. Men wasting away were making their way south, carrying with them a diagnosis most people still refused to name. On the coasts, it had a language. In Shreveport, it was only static—thin and crackling, like denial itself—until it wasn't.

Shreveport had mastered the art of looking away. AIDS was spoken of in whispers, if it was spoken of at all, as though refusing to acknowledge it could keep it from crossing the city limits. Churches remained silent, public officials looked elsewhere, and that silence became as dangerous as the virus itself.

The response was performative—a ritual of pretending, not protecting. Prayers replaced policy. Sympathy stood in for services. Churches thundered with brimstone. Doctors kept their distance. Gay men were pushed to the margins, politicians filled their calendars with everything else, and the media buried it in the back pages.

By September 1983, *The Shreveport Times* reported the region's second confirmed AIDS death, noting that the CDC was tracking additional suspected cases and that local physicians had quietly acknowledged the disease's presence. AIDS was no longer a distant coastal crisis; it was already in Shreveport-Bossier, its arrival fixed in print even as the city strained to look past it.

Two years later, in June 1985, *The Shreveport Journal* reported the parish's sixth AIDS death: a forty-one-year-old man from Nile Street who died at LSU Medical Center after more than a year of illness. The coroner confirmed eight known cases since 1983, six already dead—clear proof that a local epidemic was underway.

Public fear was growing louder than public health. In September 1985, *The Shreveport Times*—known locally simply as "The Times"— ran a front-page story titled "Strong feelings expressed here about AIDS patients in schools," capturing a community in open panic. Parents argued that children with AIDS should be kept out of classrooms; others demanded separate restrooms, isolated spaces, or removal altogether. Not a single medical expert quoted believed such measures were necessary, yet the fear persisted—a city more frightened of proximity than of ignorance. The virus was here, and Shreveport's first instinct was exclusion—not compassion.

By July 1987, the warnings could no longer be dismissed as distant possibilities. At a luncheon in Bossier City, national AIDS educator Dan Moreschi stood before civic leaders and laid out the future in stark terms: by 1991, AIDS would become the leading cause of death among American men; forty percent of those who would eventually develop the disease were already infected; and Northwest Louisiana would face a major surge in cases within five years. Reported in the *Bossier Press-Tribune*, his message insisted that AIDS was not a "gay plague," that the virus was already moving through heterosexual communities, and that the region needed to prepare immediately for treatment centers, staffing, and long-term care. The room heard him. The city did not move.

The medical record later showed what silence tried to bury. The

　　　　　　　　DR. DAVID W. HYLAN

earliest AIDS cases in Northwest Louisiana had been quietly logged at Schumpert Medical Center, Highland Hospital, and Willis-Knighton Medical Center—appearing as marginal notes rather than headlines, early evidence of a crisis the city still refused to confront. When federal AIDS relief funds finally arrived years later, most of the money stopped in New Orleans; "Northwest Louisiana shortchanged with AIDS money," a 1993 headline admitted, naming what the sick already understood: geography could decide survival.

Within Shreveport's gay community, fear had layers. To be gay was one thing; to be sick was another. Visibility carried its own peril. Even the hint of being named—by rumor, by newsprint, by association—could cost someone a job, a family, a church. In a city where survival depended on discretion, outrage had to learn to whisper before it could shout.

And in that quiet, the virus found room to breathe—and time to spread unchecked.

Funerals blurred together, one following another until grief felt like a permanent appointment on the calendar. People stopped counting because counting meant admitting how many had been lost. There was no public language for HIV, no open talk of being gay—only death and the careful omission of its cause.

Robert Darrow remembered what it felt like back then—how fear seemed to fill every room, louder than grief itself. "When people started dying from AIDS, it wasn't only the illness that haunted us. It was what came after."

Fear sealed mouths shut. People were afraid to admit illness, afraid to speak their own truth. Even in the few spaces where queer people gathered, anxiety seeped through. Euphemism became ritual: "cancer," "a long illness," "he died in his sleep." The word AIDS went unspoken even when everyone knew.

And when death came, it did not bring dignity with it.

Robert made clear this was not confined to one place. Across Northwest Louisiana—from small rural towns to Shreveport and Bossier City—funeral homes behaved much the same way, often refusing to take the bodies of those who had died from AIDS. From there, he described what families were told:

"Directors claimed the dead were still dangerous, that somehow death hadn't ended the threat. Families were told no: no service, no preparation, no goodbye. Sometimes they were told to cremate immediately.

Sometimes they were charged extra for so-called precautions—costs that made it even harder to bury their own."

The losses mounted, and with them something beneath the silence began to harden. He did not hesitate when describing what never left him from those years.

"What stayed with me most was the indignity. People I knew, people who had already suffered so much, were sometimes placed in black garbage bags by hospital staff too afraid to treat them with care. Not wrapped, not honored—contained. It felt like they were being erased even before they were buried."

Funerals, when they happened at all, were often divided in ways that were never spoken aloud. Robert described how grief itself split along those same lines. Men were mourned twice: once by their biological families, who sometimes did not know who they truly were, and again by the chosen families who had stood beside them through everything. Two separate griefs, rarely allowed to meet. Two versions of a life, kept apart even in death.

Robert did not only speak of cruelty. He also remembered what rose in response.

"But alongside that cruelty, I also witnessed something else. When institutions failed, people stepped in. Friends became family in ways that still move me when I think about it. They raised money for funerals, held benefits, made sure no one was forgotten. They cared for the dying, buried those no one else would claim, and made sure names were remembered."

It arrived without sirens, without headlines—just places left vacant at dinner tables and phones that stopped ringing. It came quietly at first, then all at once, moving through lives that had already learned how to remain unseen.

Robert described how grief refused to stay contained.

"Some funerals became acts of defiance. People carried ashes and urns into public spaces, demanding that the world acknowledge what was happening. Grief turned into protest because silence had already taken too much."

And then they were gone—not loudly, not all at once, but in rooms stripped of dignity, behind curtains drawn too tight. Death certificates told polite lies—pneumonia, cancer, heart failure—language designed to soften what no one wanted to say.

What took them was not only the virus, but everything that stepped back—the willful ignorance. What could not be named could be ignored.

　　　　　　　　　　　　　　　　DR. DAVID W. HYLAN

Those years felt like living inside a graveyard. Friends died one by one, and nearly every institution that claimed moral authority—religious, social, governmental—turned away. What survived did so not because help arrived, but because friends and chosen family built it. Living rooms became support groups. Grocery runs became food delivery networks. Hospital visits replaced sermons. Care emerged where policy failed, and love did the work that systems refused to do. Even in the depth of loss, something else took shape: a stubborn insistence on living, building, and fighting back.

The first deaths brought more than grief—they ushered in an absence so absolute it felt like a second loss. Confusion crept into living rooms and church foyers, cloaked in casseroles and murmured condolences. Shame settled like dust—undisturbed, unspoken. Mourning became private to the point of invisibility. No vigils. No public acknowledgment. Just the steady, unseen unraveling of lives in a city that refused to name the plague at its door.

In that quiet, denial proved brittle, and grief fermented into something sharper. The unspoken logic was brutal but unmistakable: the men and women dying were the ones the city had already learned to disregard.

By the late 1980s in Shreveport, that apathy and righteous moral judgment didn't just close doors—it kept the morgues full of men and women whose families often hid the truth or refused to claim the bodies. And in those years before ACT UP Shreveport formally emerged, each person who would later step into the fight experienced a private breaking point. Sometimes it happened under the fluorescent wash of the city's public hospital lights, where untouched food trays accumulated beside beds. Sometimes it arrived with a phone call confirming what everyone already feared. Sometimes it settled in during the writing of yet another obituary for someone barely thirty.

Inside the wards of LSU Medical Center, that history revealed itself in the cruelest ways. In corridors sharp with antiseptic, patients with AIDS were met not with treatment but avoidance. Some nurses refused to enter their rooms. Sheets went unchanged. Sharon Adley, a nurse at LSU, spoke quietly about what she saw, her tone marked by a kind of disbelief that this level of neglect had become routine. She recalled dirty linen piling up in bathrooms, left there for days because no one would remove it. Meals went untouched. Food trays were left on the floor outside closed doors. Gary Cathey recalled watching a staff member set a tray down in the hallway and walk away. "You just sat that on the floor," he said. The staff member responded, "Yeah, we don't go in there." Sharon also described trays left in the anteroom—breakfast and lunch piling up, never making it inside—and call bells going unanswered for hours, patients expressing relief when she finally responded after long stretches of silence. For patients too weak to stand, too sick to move, the result was simple and brutal: they went unfed. What unfolded inside LSU Medical Center was not neglect. It was starvation by avoidance.

Across town, the contrast could not have been sharper. While LSU revealed how institutional neglect could harden into policy, Schumpert Medical Center offered a different kind of story—shaped by its Catholic roots, its history of bedside care, and a quiet insistence on dignity. The two hospitals stood less than three miles apart, but for people living with AIDS in the late 1980s, they might as well have existed in different worlds.

Schumpert Medical Center on St. Mary Place occupied a complicated position in Shreveport's medical landscape. Long operated by the Sisters of Charity of the Incarnate Word, the hospital carried a Catholic identity that was conservative in culture but grounded in bedside care. During the AIDS crisis, Schumpert was often more willing than its larger counterpart to offer humane treatment to people living with HIV—care shaped less by policy than by proximity.

During the height of the epidemic in the late 1980s and early 1990s, Schumpert developed a quiet reputation for offering care that other facilities avoided. The compassion was not universal, nor was it free of fear or misinformation, but it appeared often enough to matter. Nurses stayed when others stepped back. Some physicians treated patients without spectacle or judgment. In a city where men with AIDS were routinely made to feel unwelcome, Schumpert became one of the few places where care was sometimes preserved—not as policy, but as practice. These were pockets of mercy, fragile and inconsistent, yet unforgettable to those who received them.

It was into this world that Nurse Yeona DaCosta-Auld stepped. She brought a nursing ethic shaped by Catholic training and global experience to Nine Tower, where many of the hospital's HIV/AIDS patients were admitted—arriving long after the warnings had been issued and ignored. Under the guidance of Dr. Marcus Spurlock, known to most as Marc—

one of only two physicians in Shreveport consistently treating people with AIDS—she set aside unnecessary layers of protective gear when greeting patients, choosing to meet them face-to-face rather than through plastic. Families trusted her; some waited for her shift before allowing anyone else to touch their sons. She bathed the dying, listened to their anger, and refused to let them slip away alone. In a city that often looked the other way, she treated people with dignity when others would not.

That neglect at LSU wasn't confined to hospital walls—it bled into the city itself, into streets, workplaces, and church pews. The fear wasn't just about the virus; it was about proximity—about guilt by association, about being seen with the wrong person.

It was the kind of fear that made neighbors avert their eyes, calls that never came back—a city stepping around its own people.

In the grocery store, people traded rumors about who had "that disease." At barbershops, men changed the subject when the talk came too close. Even funerals were divided—some attended in quiet support; others stayed away entirely. In Shreveport, the cure people reached for was distance.

But not everyone stepped back. Some remained. They carried food into the homes of sick friends across Shreveport when others would not. They sat by hospital beds when staff members refused to enter. They drove patients to appointments, folded laundry, scrubbed kitchens, and cared for pets left behind. They became quiet lifelines—the friends, the lovers, the chosen family—who practiced care when institutions would not.

For those living with HIV, the silence was a second diagnosis—as lethal as the first. It kept neighbors from checking in, ministers from visiting, and doctors from looking too closely. The crisis became less about the virus itself and more about whom the city believed was disposable.

And yet, across Shreveport—in driveways at dusk and at the backs of dimly lit bars—conversations began to stir. Small ones at first: whispers traded between friends, late-night conversations that stretched longer than they should, questions asked in the careful shorthand of people afraid to be overheard. But those murmurs carried heat. They pushed against the quiet that had settled over the city, pressing on the weak spots in the wall Shreveport had built around the crisis. In a place where nearly everything was spoken in code, even a single honest sentence felt dangerous. Each confession, each shared fear, made the next one easier. And in those shadowed corners—porches, parking lots, bar basements—

something unmistakable began to form: the first, faint language of resistance.

What happened at LSU was not an aberration; it was the clearest expression of a broader unwillingness to treat people with AIDS as worthy of care—a silence that followed the sick from hospital rooms into funeral homes, churches, and cemeteries.

It did not arrive in a single shattering moment. It gathered instead in low, late-night conversations—words traded after midnight over sinks full of dishes, looks that said, "I see you," and private decisions to stop pretending nothing was wrong. Grief thickened into resolve. Rage passed from hand to hand like a forbidden object—dangerous, necessary, alive.

From these small, private acts, a different kind of resistance began to breathe. It did not yet march through the streets or thunder from megaphones, but it pushed back against the cold withdrawal of care.

Stories began to circulate—unfinished, whispered, unverified. People learned who could be trusted, who could not. In a city where silence had been enforced for decades, even the act of telling the truth to one another felt radical.

It was in these tucked-away spaces—around worn kitchen tables, in parked cars, and in the back rows of community meetings where no one expected them to speak—that the seeds of confrontation were planted. As they took root, the city's quiet began to split. The murmurs that started in private rooms would soon spill outward—gaining strength.

The people who stayed—the ones who talked late into the night, who kept vigil beside hospital beds, who delivered gumbo to doorsteps when others stayed away—were building something unnamed but unmistakable. It was a refusal to let callous erasure win.

That slow-burning defiance would leave back porches and borrowed sofas and step, deliberately, into the open. The barrier of looking away would not hold forever—and when it gave way, it would not be gentle.

Shreveport had allowed silence to reign. But even here, voices were rising—toward a plan, toward a reckoning, toward something that would no longer stay hidden in back rooms or whispered conversations.

It was moving toward a table, toward a gathering, toward the moment when private anger would become shared purpose—toward dinner at George's Grill.

CHAPTER 2
DINNER AT GEORGE'S GRILL

"We were tired of watching people die. Somebody had to stand up."
—Gary Cathey, founding member of ACT UP Shreveport

By the end of the 1980s, AIDS was no longer distant or abstract in Shreveport. It had settled into daily life through omission and delay—hospital corridors that learned avoidance, churches that learned moral distance, and public offices that practiced patience while people disappeared. Funerals multiplied. People got sick, then sicker, then were gone. What the city knew, it rarely said out loud. Quiet care and private grief became the default. By 1989, those strategies were failing, and the cost could no longer be ignored.

It was in that failure that it began, as many Southern reckonings do—with a late meal taken not for comfort but because nowhere else felt possible. George's Grill, a twenty-four-hour diner on Kings Highway in Shreveport, sat wide open to the road, its plate-glass windows holding fluorescent light against the dark. Inside, the smell of bacon grease and burnt coffee clung to the air. Plates clattered. Waitresses called everyone "honey" without asking for names. When the queer bars closed, people drifted here, hungry for something steady after the music stopped.

Chuck Selber, a playwright and creative force in Shreveport; Gary Cathey, a fashion designer recently returned from New York; and Joe DeSantis, an artist and actor, sat at a table pressed close to the window, traffic sliding past as if the city were moving on without them. All three men were thin—noticeably so—the kind of change that had become familiar, though it showed differently in each of them, most clearly in Chuck, where the loss had settled into his face even beneath his beard. Chuck spoke directly, his voice rising and falling with intensity but never breaking into a yell, his disbelief sharp as he described the indignity he was witnessing—medical staff refusing to treat, to help, to even enter the rooms of people with AIDS. Gary remained composed, but just as direct, focused on what needed to happen next, unwilling to waste time now that the truth was clear. Joe moved differently, expressive and irreverent even in anger, his frustration spilling out with theatrical force, a performance shaped as much by pain as by instinct. All three carried the weight of what they had seen and lost, not just for themselves, but for a community that had been left to absorb it in silence.

George's Grill was not neutral ground, but it was forgiving ground. The noise gave cover; the windows offered visibility without exposure. At the table by the glass, grief and anger finally had somewhere to land— about hospitals that avoided them, government agencies that delayed, nonprofits that rationed care, and institutions that treated people living with HIV and AIDS as expendable.

That permission mattered because of who was sitting there. All three men were already shaped by the epidemic in different ways, carrying experience gathered far beyond Shreveport back into a city that had not yet named what it was facing. They had watched other cities move from rumor to denial to open catastrophe. They knew the pattern— how quickly hospitals filled, how families disappeared, how institutions stalled until the cost was counted in bodies. Gary spoke about it at length that night. He had seen enough in New York to understand that what was coming to Shreveport would not be mild or contained. It would be brutal. Even he underestimated how severe it would become here—how tightly silence would hold, how stubbornly local systems would resist, how many would be left to navigate illness without protection.

They did not meet for introductions. They met because each carried the same accumulation of loss and frustration. Chuck arrived from Houston with sharpened impatience, forged by watching institutions delay while people disappeared. Gary Cathey brought organizing discipline learned in New York through his volunteer work with the Gay Men's Health Crisis. Joe DeSantis, moving between coasts, had witnessed the same reckoning unfold elsewhere. What they shared that night was not novelty, but recognition—and the first pressure of something that would not stay contained.

It was late 1989. The year was closing, and the local death count was rising quietly, without ceremony. They did not arrive with a plan. They arrived carrying stories: hospital rooms no one would enter, bodies handled with gloves, funerals without families, churches that offered judgment instead of care. The conversation moved in circles at first, anger folding back on itself, grief finding no clean exit. They talked for hours until what had been unspoken finally settled between them. AIDS was not a future threat. It was already shaping daily life in Shreveport, whether the city named it or not.

This was not a meeting of strangers. Chuck, Gary, and Joe had known one another for years, their lives overlapping through shared friends, shared losses, and the small, migratory world of queer life that stretched between cities. Each had left Shreveport at different times, in different moments, chasing work, dreams, and the possibility of becoming someone else. Each had come back for reasons largely unspoken but deeply understood. By the fall of 1989, Chuck and Joe had both been diagnosed with AIDS, their illnesses already advanced. Gary believed he was sick as well, only learning much later that he was HIV-negative. All three returned home believing, in some measure, that they were coming back to die. Sitting together at George's Grill, they did not need to explain what AIDS was. What mattered was that they were all back—and that waiting had already failed them.

Even then, the idea of action felt dangerous. Shreveport was not New York. Naming AIDS in public could cost a job, a family, a church. But as the night stretched on, danger began to feel less abstract than necessity itself. If refusal was possible elsewhere, why was silence still the only option here? Gary would later say it plainly: you didn't have to be in New York to act up. You could act up anywhere. ACT UP was not a headquarters or a permission structure. It was a refusal to stay silent.

They did not leave George's Grill with a manifesto. They left with an agreement. They would stop pretending silence was harmless. They would stop waiting for institutions that had already shown they would not act in time. They did not yet know what shape the work would take, or how visible it would need to become. They only knew that what they had been doing—grieving privately, helping quietly—was no longer enough. If people were going to die anyway, they would not die unseen.

The agreement that formed that night did not arrive fully shaped. It surfaced slowly, cautiously. ACT UP—AIDS Coalition to Unleash Power. The name had already taken hold in New York and San Francisco, carried south through newsletters, phone calls, and word of mouth. There was no internet, no instant access—information moved deliberately, passed from hand to hand, voice to voice. Typed pages circulated, carrying the voices of ACT UP organizers, treatment activists, and writers—people like Larry Kramer, Michael Callen—an early AIDS activist and writer living with the disease—and Sean Strub, a publisher and organizer who would go on to found POZ magazine. By November 1989, ACT UP meant something specific: organized confrontation, public pressure, refusal to wait. That night in Shreveport, the name was spoken not as an idea, but as a decision.

The awareness hardened into something more demanding than dread. The city could still avoid the language, but it could not avoid the consequences—hospital beds filling, obituaries tightening, conversations stopping mid-sentence. What others had begun to confront openly was still being absorbed here through evasion, and the distance between knowledge and action had become intolerable. Knowing was no longer enough.

Within weeks, that commitment moved from living rooms into public record. In early 1990, *The Shreveport Journal* reported that AIDS Coalition to Unleash Power had "quietly gathered steam" in Northwest Louisiana, holding strategy sessions and weekly meetings while aligning itself with the national ACT UP network (Laura Beil, "AIDS Activists Group Forms Here," *The Shreveport Journal*). The article described the chapter as officially proclaiming itself formed during a lengthy meeting and noted that its structure remained informal—some members attending regularly, others participating only in actions. What bound them, members explained, was not hierarchy, but refusal. They rejected labels like anarchists or extremists. "We're not vigilantes," one member said. "We're citizens." Now their names were in print.

The paper also made clear what distinguished the Shreveport chapter from the national caricature of militancy. While aligned with ACT UP nationally, the local group emphasized research access and equitable treatment for people living with AIDS in Northwest Louisiana. Some of their methods were disciplined rather than theatrical: information gathering, formal letters to scientists, researchers, and politicians, extended meetings, weekly strategy sessions. It was activism shaped to fit a smaller city, where visibility carried higher cost and persuasion required persistence more than spectacle.

Each of them carried that recognition forward differently. Gary brought organizing discipline learned in New York, where he had lived and worked as a designer and volunteered with the Gay Men's Health Crisis, watching grief harden into strategy. He had seen what happened when people stopped waiting—how quickly urgency could become action when someone was willing to name it. He understood, even then, that this kind of work did not stay abstract for long. It had a way of turning inward, of becoming personal. Chuck brought creative urgency and a refusal to accept delay, shaped not only by years of watching institutions deflect responsibility while people disappeared, but by his own life increasingly affected by AIDS. Joe carried that same embodied knowledge, understanding that time was not abstract or negotiable. Together, they did not yet share a strategy, but they shared something more immediate: an understanding that waiting had become a decision of its own—and one they could no longer afford to make.

ACT UP did not arrive in Shreveport as a manual or a movement. It moved along phone lines and chance conversations—through memory and shared loss. It was carried by people who had already watched institutions delay as lives slipped away. By the time the idea took hold beyond that greasy diner table on Kings Highway, it no longer felt borrowed. ACT UP Shreveport. It felt essential.

What followed did not begin in meeting halls or public spaces. It began through trust. Conversations moved from diner tables into living rooms, from late-night phone calls into whispered invitations. Recruitment was personal. Friend to friend. Someone you knew from the gay bars. Someone who had sat beside you at a funeral. In December 1989, Deborah Allen—already embedded in the city's quiet networks of care—printed small cards, nothing flashy, nothing meant to draw attention, and slid them discreetly across tables. They did not announce a movement. They pointed to a meeting: "This is something you need to be part of." Each card carried risk. Showing up meant being seen. Being counted.

As the organizing deepened, those same networks took on structure. What began as cautious outreach became intentional recruitment. The cards turned pink, bearing the ACT UP logo, but the method stayed the same: discretion over display, trust over broadcast. Exposure still carried consequence. What changed was resolve. People began showing up not by accident, but by decision—and staying.

Gay bars carried much of the early weight of that recruitment, not as organizing sites but as connective tissue—the places people already knew one another, where news traveled before it ever reached daylight. Monty's My Way. Central Station. The Korner Lounge. Baha Beach Club. Conversations unfolded over jukebox noise and beer, invitations whispered rather than announced. Deborah passed cards there. So did others. From those rooms, recruitment flowed outward into galleries, poetry readings, and backyard gatherings—spaces where queer Shreveport intersected with sympathetic allies. Grief, creativity, and defiance mixed easily, giving the work a foothold before it took public shape.

Sometimes the invitations were almost accidental. Cecil Thad Coburn, part of the city's queer social circle, later told the story of pulling up beside Deborah at a red light. She was on her way to a funeral. In that brief exchange, she invited him to a meeting at her apartment. That was how people found one another—through funerals, bars, and chance encounters.

Robert Darrow's path into the work began earlier, and elsewhere. An actor and longtime creative force in Shreveport, Robert left Louisiana after being diagnosed HIV-positive. In a city where reputation traveled faster than compassion, he feared not only the illness but the stigma it would bring—particularly for his parents, who would be forced to carry the weight of having a son with what many still spoke of only as "that gay disease." New York offered distance—anonymity and the possibility of surviving without becoming a public spectacle at home.

In the late 1980s in Manhattan, he volunteered answering phones at Dr. Joseph Sonnabend's Community Research Initiative on AIDS, providing information and steady reassurance to callers navigating HIV and AIDS. He also attended ACT UP New York meetings at the Gay and Lesbian Community Center in the West Village, where he saw firsthand how anger was organized into strategy—how information,

　　　　DR. DAVID W. HYLAN

protest, and pressure were used deliberately to force response. There, he encountered the epidemic not as rumor, but as daily reality—the language of T-cell counts, the progression of opportunistic infections, the steady narrowing of options. As his own health deteriorated and he developed full-blown AIDS, the prognosis was blunt. He believed he had weeks, perhaps months. That belief shaped everything that followed. Robert did not study treatments out of curiosity or abstraction. He pursued them with urgency, tracking drug trials, protocols, and emerging research in a determined effort to save his own life—and, in doing so, the lives of others.

In 1989, Robert made the decision many did then: to go home to die.

Months earlier, while volunteering in New York, he had taken a call from a man in Shreveport looking for information about AIDS. The caller was Chuck Selber. They did not know each other. But when Chuck mentioned Shreveport, Robert paused. "I'm from there, too," he said. The connection lingered.

When Robert returned to Louisiana believing the end was near, he looked Chuck up and called him. Chuck told him to come to a meeting. That meeting was not a vigil. It was an organizing session. And it was there, in a room thick with urgency and grief, that Robert stepped fully into the work—not as someone new to it, but as someone who already understood what it required. With the exception of missing the now-legendary dinner at George's Grill, he would become as central to ACT UP Shreveport as Joe DeSantis, Gary Cathey, and Chuck Selber—an intricate, indispensable part of the movement's spine.

The first ACT UP Shreveport meeting, held in December 1989, took place in the apartment Deborah Allen shared with Buddy Williamson. Deborah, a hairstylist, mother, and longtime activist within Shreveport's queer community, had already been quietly holding people together for years, and most of the people who came that night had been recruited by her. Buddy, a writer and publisher, would later document much of what followed. Seven people showed up: Gary Cathey, Joe DeSantis, Chuck Selber, Deborah Allen, Buddy Williamson, Robert Darrow, and Mark Anthony Lindsey—known onstage as Marquita, one of the city's most popular drag performers.

Some arrived early, lingering on the apartment steps before knocking. Others waited until they were sure no one was watching. There was no formal agenda, no expectation of polish. What mattered was presence.

The apartment was small, an upstairs duplex, with a living room lit only by lamps and no overhead light. People filled both the living and dining areas, sitting where they could or standing along the walls.

Deborah and Buddy moved through it as hosts—Deborah calm, steady, and attentive, Buddy bringing an easy humor that helped keep the room from tightening too quickly. Snacks and drinks were set out. But beneath it was what Deborah would later describe as the perfect kind of activism: anger for the toll AIDS was taking on their friends, and love for those already living with the disease.

The tone was quiet at first—tentative, exploratory—but Chuck didn't let it stay there. He laid out the reality in direct terms: doctors refusing to treat people with AIDS and hospitals responding with fear instead of care. Robert recalled taking a friend, Vern Ransburg, to a doctor who refused to see him because he had AIDS. Chuck pressed further—LSU Medical Center was not applying for or participating in experimental drug trials, and access to treatment that might extend lives was being withheld. He was furious that the Greater Louisiana Alliance for Dignity (later renamed Greater Louisiana AIDS Defense, GLAD), the only AIDS awareness organization in the area, was not fighting for that access. If they would not act, he said, then ACT UP would—and that might mean confronting not only institutions, but members of their own community willing to look the other way.

Chuck, Robert, and Gary described what they had seen in New York—how ACT UP used confrontation and deliberate, often theatrical disruption to force attention and change. Media mattered. Pressure mattered. Exposure mattered. Chuck made it clear he was willing to use all of it, including arrest if necessary. What began as an introduction to what ACT UP could be sharpened into a challenge. Do whatever was necessary. Expose the system. The mood in the room held that tension: grief already present, and something like hope rising alongside it.

The second meeting, held in January 1990 in the apartment Deborah Allen shared with Buddy Williamson, drew fourteen people. The growth was immediate, but so was the shift in tone. What had begun as an exploratory conversation became more focused, more deliberate. The recent actions at GLAD and the Northwest Louisiana AIDS Task Force—both of which had drawn front-page coverage in *The Shreveport Journal*—hung over the room. Some faces showed concern about the exposure. Others were energized by it.

Discussions moved quickly from frustration to action. Issues were named. Responses were debated. Creative strategies were proposed—not just what to say, but how to force people to listen. They discussed where the meetings would continue, including Shoney's and eventually the B'nai Zion temple. There were no formal votes. Decisions emerged through consensus, shaped by urgency more than procedure. People took on responsibilities based on what they were willing to do. If an action felt like too much, you stepped back. If not, you stepped forward.

By the third meeting later that same month, thirty-five people gathered at Chuck's family home. The space was tight, and the growth was unmistakable. What had begun as a small, cautious gathering was quickly becoming something larger—something that could no longer be contained in a single room. For many, it was the first time they realized they were not alone—not just in grief, but in anger. The growth was not accidental. It answered a need that had been waiting for a place to land.

That growth carried a cost. Not everyone welcomed the organizing. Pushback came quickly, sometimes from within the same community the group hoped to mobilize. People questioned whom ACT UP claimed to speak for. Others feared that showing up meant being labeled—political, sick, or both.

The resistance was not always abstract. Gary Cathey received death threats from neighbors in nearby Minden, Louisiana, warning that visibility carried consequences beyond meetings and headlines—beyond the movement itself. Deborah Allen was confronted directly by a local nursing home director, who called her a "freak" and accused her of putting others at risk—an accusation shaped as much by fear as by prejudice.

The resistance extended beyond isolated encounters. In bars and public spaces, some within the gay community responded with visible judgment—stares that lingered, conversations that stopped when ACT UP members entered, a quiet but unmistakable distancing from those who refused to stay silent. At political offices, protests sometimes prompted calls to the police, forcing members out of private spaces and into public view.

Institutional resistance carried even higher stakes. At LSU Medical Center, discussions included proposals as extreme as installing exhaust systems to remove contaminated air—an idea rooted more in fear than science. Doctors refused to treat patients. These were not abstract barriers. They were decisions, made in real time, with immediate consequences.

The same spaces that offered cover could also expose them. A pink card slid across a napkin could mark someone as an activist—or worse, as positive. For some, the risk outweighed the urgency. They stopped coming—and their absence made clear who would remain.

By late 1989 and into the opening months of 1990, that early phase of organizing revealed who would stay. As AIDS deaths continued to rise in Caddo and Bossier parishes and access to AZT remained uncertain and uneven, some people drifted away—frightened by visibility, exhausted by the weight of it all. Others leaned in harder. They understood this was not symbolic resistance. It was survival work, unfolding in real time, with consequences measured in bodies and days.

That commitment reshaped how the work had to be done. As weekly meetings continued, shared urgency hardened into discipline. Chuck came prepared with agendas and to-do lists, guiding discussions toward decisions rather than reflection. Issues were raised, strategies debated, and responsibilities assigned before the meeting ended. People were expected to follow through—writing letters, making phone calls, showing up where they were needed.

The resistance they faced from within the queer community was not incidental—it became a recurring point of discussion at nearly every meeting. The frustration ran deep. They were taking risks, making themselves visible, pushing for change that would benefit everyone, and in return they were met with distance, criticism, or outright hostility. For some in the room, that rejection cut sharply. Chuck had little patience for it. If others chose silence, that was their decision—but it would not slow ACT UP's mission.

The structure did not announce itself all at once—it revealed itself through repetition. Meetings began to follow a pattern: an issue raised, a response shaped, a plan set in motion before anyone left the room. Deborah continued distributing the cards—simple, blank-backed, meant to be passed from hand to hand, with each person filling in the details of the next meeting: a time, an address, a phone number. They became small, deliberate extensions of the work. What held the group together was not formality, but follow-through. People came back. They did what they said they would do. And the work kept moving.

Chuck drove that shift more insistently than anyone. A writer and creative force who had lived and worked in New York—and who was himself living with AIDS—Chuck returned to Shreveport carrying both experience and impatience. He did not arrive quietly. He came with urgency sharpened by time he no longer believed he had.

Chuck was determined to keep meetings from dissolving into abstraction or catharsis alone. He pressed for clarity: what was the goal, who was responsible, what would happen next. When conversations drifted, he pulled them back to consequence—who was dying, where delays were occurring, which institutions were hiding behind procedure. It was not cruelty. It was triage. It was time, measured against the body.

Meetings moved wherever space could be borrowed without drawing attention—apartments and family homes at first, then repeatedly to a Shoney's restaurant, where gatherings could take place without scrutiny, before eventually moving into a room at B'nai Zion Temple on Southfield Road, where doors could close without judgment. The locations changed, but the tone did not. This was work, and it had to move.

Authority emerged through action rather than title. People left meetings knowing what they were responsible for—who needed to be called, which hospital administrator required pressure, what information had to be gathered before the next meeting. Participation now required follow-through. Those who stayed understood that what lay ahead would demand more than presence. It would demand persistence.

Others carved out roles that mattered just as much. Robert Darrow, who brought both creative sensibility and a deepening medical knowledge shaped by his own diagnosis, became a stabilizing presence in the room. He brought medical updates to meetings, summarized treatment trials, and translated emerging data into language people could use. His file folders became fixtures, grounding urgency in information and keeping anger from tipping into chaos. Outrage, he reminded them, worked best when it was armed with facts. Information was not comfort. It was leverage.

Deborah Allen, one of the group's earliest and most tireless organizers, took on the work of logistics and sustainability. She ordered shirts and posters from ACT UP New York, including a Keith Haring print she would later keep, organized small fundraisers, and handled the details that made the work possible but rarely visible. Cecil Thad Coburn moved more quietly. He was not the loudest voice in the room or the most constant presence, but he showed up when he could, steady in the background. His role underscored that commitment. It did not always announce itself.

Creative labor carried its own authority. Chris Free, a graphics designer and typesetter, helped shape ACT UP Shreveport's visual identity, designing posters and graphics and painting sweatshirts with bold logos that became an unofficial uniform. Kenny King, an artist and drag performer, and Kurt Pickett, often the youngest in the room and later an academic who would earn his doctorate, brought wit, intellect, and theatrical flair into the movement, blending humor with defiance in ways that drew attention without dilution. Alana Oldham, also among the youngest, brought a sharp, steady presence into the work—observant, engaged, and unwilling to stay in the background. Chad Cromer moved within that same orbit, another young voice shaped by the moment and part of the energy pushing the work forward. Buddy Williamson carried the work outward, documenting ACT UP's message beyond meeting rooms and into bars, living rooms, and kitchens across the city through his newsletter, *Tri-State Tea*.

As visibility increased, misunderstandings followed. Some assumed ACT UP functioned like a charity. Thad even opened a bank account in its name. Reality corrected that quickly. There was very little money, and Chuck often covered expenses himself. The work was not about easing discomfort or offering services. It was about applying pressure. That distinction mattered. ACT UP was not there to soften institutions. It was there to force them into action.

As Chuck stayed in contact with ACT UP New York and other chapters, information flowed back like dispatches from the front—tactics, language, lessons learned. What emerged in Shreveport was not imitation, but adaptation. Discipline, roles, and escalation took shape within the constraints of a smaller city, where visibility carried higher personal cost and retreat was often safer than confrontation. What they borrowed was not style, but insistence.

By this point, ACT UP Shreveport was no longer a loose gathering held together by grief alone. It had developed muscle memory. Meetings produced assignments. Assignments produced action. Action demanded escalation. The tone was set—controlled, relentless, unwilling to accept delay. With that discipline in place, the group turned outward, shifting from organizing itself to confronting the institutions that had failed them—and continued to.

The first action came quickly.

At George's Grill, Chuck had already made clear where his frustration was aimed. He had been trying to get movement from the AIDS Task Force on access to experimental drug trials and getting nowhere. But his anger did not stop there. In a city with only one organization providing AIDS-related prevention services, he could not understand why the Greater Louisiana Alliance for Dignity (GLAD) was not pushing harder—why it was not demanding access to treatments that might keep people alive.

So, ACT UP went to GLAD and asked the question directly.

They did not arrive quietly. Chuck had already contacted a reporter and photographer, knowing the confrontation would not stay contained. If the conversation would not move behind closed doors, it would be forced into the open.

They were pushed out of the meeting and into the view of a reporter and photographer.

The confrontation did not end there. Within days, ACT UP carried that same demand into a meeting with the AIDS Task Force, pressing for access to experimental drug trials that remained out of reach for patients in Northwest Louisiana. The room did not empty. People stayed in their seats, waiting for something to shift that never did. Questions were answered slowly, if at all. What ACT UP encountered was not urgency, but process—layers of explanation that did not change the outcome. Access was still limited. Time was still passing.

They left with something clearer than resolution: the system would not move without pressure.

That shift produced immediate results. Phone trees formed and tightened. Information moved faster than rumor—sometimes faster than institutions could contain it. When calls were ignored, people showed up. ACT UP members began appearing at board meetings, hospital offices, public meetings, health department briefings, and administrative spaces where they were not invited and did not wait to be acknowledged. They demanded time. They pressed for answers, refusing deferral to committees or future agendas. Agencies accustomed to quiet compliance were forced to respond in front of witnesses rather than behind paperwork.

As that presence solidified, internal roles sharpened without formal assignment. Some handled logistics, tracking meetings, calls, and follow-ups. Others focused on outreach, expanding the circle at bars, art spaces, and community events. A few became translators, turning medical language into something neighbors could use—and anger into demands delivered face to face.

And then there was Chuck. Not louder than the others, not always gentler, but unmistakable. When discussions stalled or drifted toward caution, he pulled them back to who was dying. Where. Why. What was being delayed under the cover of procedure.

From the inside, the work was anything but disorganized. Bryan Sullivan, a hairstylist who would later become a successful business owner, remembered it clearly: Chuck ran the meetings, and everyone left knowing what they were supposed to do. Deborah described a rhythm shaped by necessity rather than rule. Decisions were usually blunt: "This is what we're going to do. If you don't want to, fine." They arrived through consensus rather than formal votes. Agreement mattered more than process. Urgency and improvisation carried more weight than procedure.

What emerged from those early months of organizing was not chaos, but resolve. ACT UP Shreveport became disciplined without becoming rigid, urgent without becoming reckless. The group understood that delay itself was deadly—and that refusing it, again and again, whether by phone, in meetings, or face to face, was the work.

Disagreements did occur, but they were not the norm. Most meetings moved with a shared sense of purpose, shaped more by urgency than division. At times, tensions surfaced around tactics or timing. Chuck pushed for bolder action. Gary urged caution. Robert steadied the room with measured assessments. Kurt brought persuasion and creativity into the conversation. These moments did not fracture the group. Meetings might end in exhaustion, but rarely in paralysis. What held them together was momentum—and the shared knowledge that stopping meant someone paid for it.

That momentum did not stay contained. ACT UP Shreveport became known for refusing to wait its turn. Members showed up where they were not invited and were not expected. They demanded time. They pressed for answers. They refused deferral to committees or future agendas. Institutions accustomed to quiet compliance found themselves confronted—sometimes abruptly, sometimes repeatedly, but always in public.

This was not spectacle for its own sake. It was insistence. ACT UP documented failures, tracked promises, and returned with evidence. When agencies claimed constraints, members asked who had set those limits and who was being left behind by them. When officials tried to

　　　　　DR. DAVID W. HYLAN

move on, ACT UP stayed in the room. Persistence replaced permission, and visibility became leverage.

That persistence carried particular weight in Shreveport. This was not New York or San Francisco. Here, silence had long been enforced by social cost. Speaking out could cost work, family, or faith. ACT UP's refusal demonstrated that the same stance—refusal, repetition, accountability—could be applied in hospital corridors, public health offices, and municipal spaces in Northwest Louisiana.

In that sense, ACT UP Shreveport became part of a larger argument. Local action was not a lesser version of national resistance but its necessary counterpart. The same delays challenged in Washington were challenged here—across desks, in fluorescent-lit rooms, under the steady hum of air conditioning. The same lives, weighed against indifference in real time. What happened in Shreveport mattered because it confirmed something essential: the AIDS crisis did not belong to any one city, and neither did the fight against it.

What set this organizing apart was not simply that it happened, but how it was held together. From the beginning, Chuck treated the work as urgent and unfinished. These were not therapy sessions, though grief was everywhere. They were not social gatherings, though friendship often filled the room. Each meeting had a point, and Chuck guarded it. When conversations drifted toward comfort, he pulled them back to the stakes. Silence, he believed, was not neutral. It was lethal.

That insistence changed the temperature of the work. What had once felt fragile hardened into something sustained. This was not a phase or a gesture, but a confrontation meant to last. The pressure was landing. Institutions felt it. So did the people doing the work. It demanded leadership that did not flinch at conflict and understood anger not as loss of control, but as fuel—aimed with precision and carried at personal cost.

That role did not emerge through vote or title. It emerged through gravity. By the early months of 1990, Chuck occupied the center of the work because the work required what he carried: focus sharpened by grief, impatience honed into strategy, and an unwillingness to let comfort masquerade as compassion. Where others hesitated, he counted what delay would cost. Where others saw obstacles, he saw leverage.

By the end of that first stretch of organizing, something irreversible had taken hold. ACT UP Shreveport was no longer a borrowed name or an idea spoken in hope. It was a presence. With that presence came a reckoning the city could no longer avoid.

But inside the movement, another reckoning was already underway—one carried most visibly by Chuck. What drove him was not impatience alone, but something sharper, more deliberate, more dangerous to ignore—what became Chuck Selber's purposeful anger.

CHAPTER 3
CHUCK SELBER'S PURPOSEFUL ANGER

"Where's the compassion and love for thy neighbor? The silence is deafening. The silence is killing us."
—Chuck Selber, founding member of ACT UP Shreveport

The spirit of ACT UP did not stop at state lines. Its energy leapt from city to city, finding new voices, new leaders, and new battlegrounds. When it reached Shreveport and Northwest Louisiana in the late 1980s—far from the coastal cities where headlines were written—it had to adapt. The South resisted not just change, but the conversations that could save lives. In that resistance, the fight took on a different shape, hardened by silence.

Before the marches, before the confrontations and headlines, that work began in a single room. Chuck Selber, a Shreveport native living with AIDS, was bent over a desk in a bedroom at his mother's mid-century ranch house on Camellia Lane, just behind Pierremont Mall. The house was comfortable and well-kept, carrying the quiet familiarity of a family that had lived there for years. The room held stacks of papers in precarious piles, the steady clatter of a word processor and dot-matrix printer filling the air. The furnishings were ordinary—a bed, dresser, desk—walls lined with photographs and artwork he had chosen for himself. The door was usually open. His mother checked on him from time to time. He worked mostly alone, not in chaos but in focus, pages and notes arranged in careful order. Chuck's body was failing, but his mind moved quickly as time closed in. He was often hunched over his desk or working from bed, as sitting upright became harder to sustain. His speech had begun to fail him, words coming with effort, sometimes difficult to understand, but the urgency behind them never dimmed.

That urgency did not stay contained. Local reporters began to take notice. In 1990, *The Shreveport Journal* described "a sick man with a typewriter and a telephone who refused to go quietly," noting that Selber's letters and press releases often reached their desks before the morning coffee cooled. He wrote until the ribbon ink ran dry, warning that neglect at the city's hospitals and delays in Louisiana's participation in national drug trials would cost lives. Private fury became public record.

This was not improvisation. Long before the attention arrived, Chuck had learned how power listened—where it stalled, and where it could be forced to respond. Having worked as an executive representing celebrity clients in New York, he understood access. He wrote formal letters and made daily calls to pharmaceutical companies, media outlets, and members of Congress, determined to reach someone who could no longer look away—corporate executive, newspaper editor, or U.S. senator. He kept lists—names, numbers, points to make—often writing out exactly what he would say before picking up the phone. Nothing was left to chance.

He tapped out speeches, revised drafts, and edited every word with urgency. In that bedroom, he produced statements, letters, and talking points meant to travel far beyond the house.

Chuck was born in Shreveport, Louisiana. When he was diagnosed with AIDS in the late 1980s, the news came in guarded tones, in conversations no one wanted to have.

It was his sister, Kay Zeidman, who told their parents. The words came out in fragments, but their mother, Flo, and father, Irving, did not flinch. Flo absorbed it with a steadiness that held the family in place. She moved deliberately, spoke carefully, and held herself with a quiet optimism that did not draw attention to itself but steadied the room. What they heard was not just a diagnosis, but a sentence—one that, in Shreveport, carried the weight of judgment and an almost certain outcome.

Flo Selber's response did not remain private for long. In July 1990,

   DR. DAVID W. HYLAN

she began organizing MAP—Mothers of AIDS Patients—a support group for mothers of children living with AIDS or lost to the disease. They met quietly, often without announcement. As a member's child died, the mother would often simply stop coming. The circle did not grow so much as it turned over, marked by absence as much as presence.

Chuck refused to let it win. His anger was purposeful and unashamed. He pushed people harder than they thought they could go, demanding that even private conversations match the stakes of a plague.

Richard Kightlinger, an artist and early ACT UP Shreveport member, saw that pressure up close. Chuck, he said, "had a way of pushing people into the fire, even when they weren't sure they could stand the heat. He would ask me to come to things I didn't even know how to maneuver through. But with Chuck, you didn't say no. He made you believe you had to be there—that showing up mattered. It was abrasive, yes, but never for its own sake. Chuck's relentlessness was always aimed at truth, never at comfort."

Judy Williams, an ACT UP Shreveport member, lived in a Shreveport where reputation carried weight. As the founder of Williams Creative Group, a respected marketing and public relations firm in Northwest Louisiana, she was visible in a city that rewarded conformity and punished deviation. Among her many honors, she was named a recipient of the 2000 ATHENA Leadership Award, a distinction that marked her as one of the city's most respected voices.

Her connection to ACT UP Shreveport did not begin with strategy or ideology. It began with Chuck Selber. They had been friends since junior high, and when he returned home with AIDS, that friendship drew her into the movement through something more immediate than politics—loyalty, witness, and love.

She showed up where she was needed—at fundraisers, at protests, in the quiet and public spaces where attention was being demanded. And after Chuck's death, when many drifted away, she did not disappear. Her activism continued, shaped by the same core principles that defined Chuck and ACT UP: speak up, show up, refuse silence.

At one point, she organized a group of women to publicly challenge what she saw as inequitable treatment of queer people and the political indifference surrounding the AIDS crisis, including the voting record of Congressman Jim McCrary. It was not a retreat from the work, but a continuation of it—carried forward in her own voice.

When she thought of Chuck, it was not anger that came first.

"No," she said. "He had a wonderful sense of humor. He made me laugh... even at the end. He was just delightful."

The anger was real. But it was never the whole of him.

By 1990, the effects of the disease were becoming harder to ignore. Chuck's weight dropped. Fatigue set in more quickly, and periods of strength grew shorter. He continued working, but the pace came at a cost. What he pushed outward in energy, his body was beginning to take back.

As the months passed, that balance shifted. There were days when getting out of bed required negotiation with a body that no longer followed his lead. Even then, the work did not stop. Letters continued. The calls did too, even as the margin for endurance narrowed.

When life carried him to New York City in the years before AIDS reshaped public life there, Chuck absorbed lessons that would later define his fight in Shreveport. He saw how grief could be turned into spectacle, how silence could be shattered with intention, how even funerals could be transformed into protest. He was not a visible activist during those years. What New York gave him was preparation—fury stored like kindling, waiting for a spark.

After leaving New York, he spent time in Houston with his sister Kay and her family as his health worsened. In October 1988, as his illness progressed, Chuck returned to Shreveport, carrying the urgency he had absorbed in Manhattan's meeting halls back to Louisiana. That duality—small-town son with big-city resolve—gave Chuck's voice uncommon weight. He could speak to men in suits and mothers in pews, to national networks and local papers that still refused to print the word "AIDS." Wherever he stood, he returned to the same truth: silence was the enemy.

Chuck, Gary, and Joe returned to Shreveport under the same shadow—each carrying loss, each unwilling to remain silent. By then, Chuck and Joe had progressed from HIV to AIDS, and Gary, convinced he was HIV-positive, came home expecting to die with his family, because in those days a diagnosis felt like a verdict.

Gary described their bond as a shared disgust—at how people with AIDS were treated, and at the silence surrounding it. Silence about transmission, funding, and responsibility. What bound them was the certainty that remaining quiet was not neutral; it was killing people they loved.

Flo later described what that neglect looked like in practice. In all of Shreveport, there was only one pharmacy that carried AZT. Dentists refused to treat patients with AIDS. Even their ophthalmologist would only see Chuck after hours, when other patients wouldn't know.

When Robert returned to Shreveport, he reconnected with Chuck—two men already aligned in urgency, each bringing a different kind of force into the work.

Chuck wasn't interested in cautious meetings or polite appeals. From the start, he pushed for actions that would disrupt comfort and force attention, insisting the system had to be shocked to move. Bryan Sullivan, a close friend and creative collaborator who would become an early ACT UP Shreveport member, said Chuck "was in your face, not to be ignored." The style could be abrasive, but it cut through hesitation. No one left the room unclear about where Chuck stood or what he demanded.

Organization followed quickly. He sent newsletters, drafted statements, and began shaping what would become ACT UP Shreveport. His family's living room served as both workspace and gathering place—papers spread across coffee tables, phones ringing, chairs pulled close—where letters were written, calls were made, and early meetings took shape before the group found permanent ground.

Chuck didn't wait for the world to care. He forced it—through writing, physical presence, and actions that demanded attention. In a city that dared not whisper the word "AIDS," he said it aloud, again and again, claiming it not as an abstraction but as his own lived reality. He spoke as someone whose body carried the stakes of every delay and denial. In classrooms, hospital auditoriums, and candlelit vigils, he spoke as if the world were on fire—because, to him, it already was.

Being Jewish shaped the rhythm of his fight. He understood activism not only as politics, but as obligation. At a Holocaust memorial service in Shreveport, when gay people were excluded from the list of victims, Chuck rose and lifted a pink triangle in quiet protest. It was a deliberate refusal of erasure—an insistence that memory could not be selective. He carried history in his bones, and he recognized what silence could do when a society chose comfort over witness.

Back in Shreveport, he became the engine that kept the movement running when energy flagged, the irritant who refused ease, the conscience of ACT UP Shreveport as it took shape. As Cecil Thad Coburn said, ACT UP Shreveport was Chuck's brainchild. "He was more radical than any of us. He was always pushing to move faster." Without Chuck's fury and vision, there might not have been an ACT UP in Shreveport at all.

He fought to secure public ground for confrontation, convincing B'nai Zion Temple, a Shreveport synagogue, to host meetings. At one gathering, as frustration mounted over the lack of urgency—even within the group—Chuck's anger broke through. He struck a hanging light fixture, shattering it. The room went still. No one moved. It wasn't destruction for its own sake—it was a desperate demand for movement, a refusal to accept that even here, energy could falter while people were dying. That urgency did not stay contained. At home, in moments when the weight of it all closed in, he broke a plate glass door—another expression of the same desperation, a body and mind pushing against limits that would not yield.

It was a refusal to let complacency dim the urgency of a plague.

Chuck carried that same confrontational instinct into local institutions, refusing to let decisions remain hidden behind closed doors. Where others accepted delay, he forced visibility—bringing pressure, attention, and consequence into rooms that had long operated without it.

Coverage did more than report conflict; it carried a plea. Editorial pages urged the city toward compassion, acknowledging that prejudice in hospitals and politics was costing lives. For the first time, mainstream Shreveport echoed what Chuck had been shouting for years—demands no longer dismissible as fringe or extreme.

That reach extended beyond the city. In New Orleans, Chuck helped organize a major civil disobedience action protesting cuts to AIDS funding—bodies in the street, arrests by design. It was classic ACT UP, deliberate and unafraid, and through that action he ensured Northwest Louisiana was not absent from a fight that had become regional and national.

But Chuck wasn't only fire. He was wit—sharp, theatrical, precisely timed to puncture cruelty when grief threatened to suffocate everything else. On the Strand stage, at a fundraiser, he turned judgment into spectacle, snatching the toupee from the head of a man who had dismissed him, exposing the performance beneath the piety. At a local hibachi restaurant, already thin and visibly worn, he insisted on being there, refusing to let illness shrink the shape of his life. When a chef, half-joking, pointed at him and said he needed to eat more, Chuck didn't deflect or soften it. "I have AIDS," he said, evenly, without apology. The room stilled. The rhythm of knives and laughter faltered. Then, just as quickly, he added, "Don't worry. I can't give it to you from over here." A nervous laugh moved through the table, but the moment had already shifted. His humor had teeth. It wasn't escape; it was confrontation delivered with timing, daring people to laugh and think at the same time.

Long before his illness progressed, he had already shown that instinct, briefly pulling Shreveport into Broadway's orbit by initiating and organizing "*A Party with Debbie Reynolds*," a 1988 benefit that raised funds for the Northwest Louisiana AIDS Task Force and the Greater Louisiana AIDS Defense—one of the first successful AIDS fundraisers to bring together the broader community.

As his body weakened, those who loved him noticed the shift. Speech grew harder. Strength faded. But the work continued. Even from his bed, Chuck pushed calls, drafts, and plans forward. Friends saw his room not as retreat, but as a nerve center. ACT UP had taught him that every act mattered. Flat on his back, he dictated and edited, imagining the next move. What others saw as stubbornness was survival.

There were other traces of him that didn't belong to the public fight. For a time, he kept two cats—Lithium and Lateral, black and white companions who moved with him from New York to Houston. When his health declined and he could no longer care for them, he gave them to his sister, Kay and her family. The loss lingered. Afterward, he kept two stuffed cats that looked just like them. He held them close when he was in bed, especially in the long stretches when the body began to win. Years later, those same worn shapes passed through the family, becoming toys for dogs and then granddogs—small, quiet artifacts of a life that had once held both fury and tenderness at the same time.

Deborah Allen remembered those days not as strategy, but as friendship—sitting with Chuck as he helped her with college papers, insisting she think harder even as his body failed. Tenderness threaded through fury. The family rotated through the house. Flo kept vigil. She held his hand and spoke to him softly, steady in a way that did not allow fear to take over the room.

Love became labor.

James Smith, a nurse, an early ACT UP Shreveport member, and one of Chuck's closest collaborators—often a pot stirrer when conversations stalled—sat beside him for hours, listening as Chuck spoke about what still needed to happen. "It's where I saw him at his most raw and fearless," James said. Even then, Chuck demanded honesty. Words had to land hard. Time could not be wasted.

Ashley Hazelton was very young, watching all of this through the example of her mother, Deborah Allen, and her brother, Micah Harold, as they took active roles in ACT UP Shreveport. Chuck sometimes babysat her, folding ordinary care into a life already crowded with urgency. He often promised to take her to the movies—small promises, repeated, familiar. Then one day, gently, he told her he couldn't make good on them. Ashley understood, even then, what he was saying. It was the moment she realized Chuck knew he was going to die soon.

In the days before his death, Chuck lay in the hospital, already slipping beyond conversation. Flo did not meet grief with spectacle. She met it the way she met everything else—with steadiness. Those who knew her understood the difference immediately. Where others reached for emotion, Flo reached for clarity. She accepted what was happening not because it was bearable, but because it was real.

In the hospital, the ending did not feel confined to a single moment. People came and went, moving through the room in quiet succession, each carrying their own version of goodbye.

Kay remembered the distance in him. When she sat beside him, she did not try to draw him back with questions. She asked him to squeeze her hand if he could hear her. That was how she spoke to him then—through touch, through presence, through words that may or may not have reached him. Most of it was her voice, steady, filling the space where his could no longer answer.

Flo was there, but not in a way that called attention to itself. She did not claim the moment or shape it into something it wasn't. She remained as she had always been—present, composed, unwilling to turn grief into performance.

Later, trying to explain what that kind of loss becomes, Flo said something that stayed with those who heard it. It was not about Chuck directly, but it was understood. Grief, she said, is like wearing a second skin.

It does not come off. It does not loosen. It does not announce itself every moment. But it is always there.

The long decline had already made the outcome clear. Those closest to him understood what was coming. Irving was with him at the end. Flo

     DR. DAVID W. HYLAN

stepped out briefly for lunch, expecting to return in time. She didn't. By the time she came back, he was gone.

For years, that absence stayed with her. The weight of stepping out, of not being there in that final moment, settled quietly and did not leave. It softened only later, when her daughter-in-law Phyllis told her, "You were with Chuck when he came into the world, and Pop was with him when he left this world." Flo carried that thought with her. It completed the circle—and brought her peace.

By the time he died, he had already woven Shreveport into the national fight—its name now spoken alongside cities that refused silence. His absence left a vacuum, but not emptiness. What remained was a blueprint. The language, the methods, the courage settled into muscle memory.

He was the backbone—the one who made the calls, pushed the fights, and believed ACT UP gave him something to fight when the virus itself could not be fought directly.

He was loved—fierce and kind. His family remembered the boy beneath the firebrand. Friends remembered how he made them braver. Robert Darrow said Chuck was "possibly awkward at times, but with his heart always in the right place."

After he was gone, the work did not stop. It changed shape. Grief moved outward, looking for somewhere to go—for a way to be seen, named, and held. What had once been carried by one voice now had to be carried by many, turning outward toward the city itself, toward the institutions that had failed, and toward the daily, unrelenting fights that defined survival.

The movement would no longer be driven by one man's force, but by many battles unfolding at once—by what became local struggles.

CHAPTER 4
LOCAL STRUGGLES

"It was never about being polite. It was about being heard."
—Robert Darrow, ACT UP Shreveport member

The fight for dignity in Shreveport was not waged on stages history books easily remember. It unfolded in quieter, meaner places—hospital corridors where trays of food were left outside doors, state offices where legislators sneered or turned away, and small-town restaurants where ACT UP members slid into booths and refused to move. Inside the hospitals, Dr. Marcus "Marc" Spurlock saw the same neglect. A formidable force, he knew the rules but made them work for patients rather than the other way around. He was unapologetically blunt and direct—enough that some feared him—but he was also the region's leading authority on HIV/AIDS treatment, deeply respected by both patients and colleagues. He forced change by firing nurses who mistreated AIDS patients, making it clear that cruelty would cost staff their jobs. He also called out the hypocrisy when administrators suddenly wanted more patients—because, as he said flatly, HIV care had become a "cash cow." It was its own form of protest, carried out with authority from inside the system.

ACT UP Shreveport moved through the world in two ways: one built, the other confronted. An initiative gathered—raising money when there was none, holding space for grief, and educating neighbors who did not yet understand. It held that community together in borrowed rooms filled with music and art, sustaining the effort and making continued action possible. An action named a target, stepping into public view to disrupt comfort and demand change, carrying a demand to a specific institution while refusing to be ignored. If an initiative built the foundation, an action tested the walls.

Before ACT UP Shreveport took to the streets, it learned how to sustain itself. Activism required more than outrage; it required infrastructure. In October 1989, Enoch's Auction gathered artists, organizers, and volunteers to raise urgently needed funds in a city offering little support. In November, Fashion Uphoria expanded that effort, raising money while building visible community in a place where visibility carried risk.

At the same time, Artists' AIDS Response emerged as a coordinated cultural effort, bringing painters, performers, playwrights, and musicians into alignment with the crisis. In December 1989, Cabaret Blasé unfolded alongside an AIDS-related art exhibition at All Souls Unitarian Universalist Church and later at Enoch's, blending music, performance, and remembrance. It did not operate as a protest arm but as a cultural amplifier, raising funds while insisting that AIDS was a lived presence in Shreveport's creative community.

The pattern continued in October 1990 with *Slave to Fashion*, a large-scale fundraiser that converted Central Station, a gay bar in Shreveport, into a runway and financed the work. Around the same period, the *Outrageous Wearable Art* fashion show brought designers, models, and musicians together to raise operational funds while expanding ACT UP's reach. In December, *Cabaret Florentine,* the first Annual Auction Against AIDS, offered another evening of gathering and support, raising money while giving a fatigued community space to breathe.

On November 29, 1991, the movement entered East Ridge Country Club. The auction and fashion show, organized by Deborah Allen, Kenny King, Joe DeSantis, Alana Oldham, Kurt Pickett, Jody Sands, and Penny Crevoiserat, carried meaning beyond the funds it generated. AIDS activism moved into a setting associated with wealth and distance from the epidemic, disrupting assumptions about who it belonged to. The use of drag queens as models raised eyebrows, and one designer reportedly lost her job as a result.

These initiatives built the networks that made sustained action possible. Without them, confrontation would have burned out.

Not every action unfolded at a podium or beneath a banner. Some took shape in daily acts—stubborn, repeated, and often unrecorded. Before confrontation defined the relationship between the Greater Louisiana Alliance for Dignity and ACT UP Shreveport or rope stretched across bridges, it lived in hospital rooms and quiet refusals. On Nine Tower at Schumpert, nurse Yeona DaCosta-Auld turned daily care into resistance. Trained in India and seasoned in hospitals across the Middle East, she arrived in Shreveport carrying both skill and spine. She refused to treat patients as untouchable. When others lingered in doorways, double-gloved and masked behind layers of plastic precaution, Yeona walked in steady and unarmored. She sat beside the furious and the frightened. She bathed the dying. Families learned to time their visits to her shift, trusting that when she was on the floor, their loved ones would be handled with gentleness rather than suspicion. Some families became far more cooperative and at ease when Yeona was involved, not because she could prevent every procedure, but because she showed them how to remain present in love rather than retreat in fear. Patients and families felt relief when she entered the room. Where others performed care mechanically, if at all, Yeona worked with compassion, speaking to patients and teaching those around them how to show tenderness without panic. In a city that preferred distance, Yeona's presence became its own protest.

It grew in improvised ways, built out of necessity rather than design.

In 1985, as fear outran information and local institutions hesitated, a small group of Shreveport residents formed the Greater Louisiana Alliance for Dignity. Among the early founders were Joe Hudson and his partner, Johnny Benson, owners of the Fun Shop; hotelier David Dement, son of a former Bossier City mayor; and Rev. Terry DeMarco of the Metropolitan Community Church. There were no grants or infrastructure—only personal donations and urgency.

That fall, while completing his master's degree at the University of Alabama at Birmingham, Mical DeBrow was contacted by David Dement and asked to present the latest scientific information about AIDS to the fledgling organization. What began as an educational session became deeper involvement. By late 1985, he was serving as its first elected chair.

GLAD did not begin with formal organization. That came under

Mical's leadership: an operational board reporting monthly to members, and membership defined by a signed confidentiality pledge protecting the identities of people living with HIV. Under IRS regulations governing its new 501(c)(3) status, GLAD focused on education and social services, with political activity prohibited. Early funding arrived through a grant from the NO/AIDS Task Force, a critical but restrictive lifeline.

The organization eventually changed its name to Greater Louisiana AIDS Defense, a shift recommended by Mical and approved by membership vote. The intention was to broaden its focus beyond lesbian and gay populations and present a more inclusive public identity in a climate already hostile to association with homosexuality.

The work was not insulated from danger. During his tenure as chair, Mical's home was broken into. He was beaten and threatened, and his position at Schumpert Medical Center was jeopardized. Facing escalating intimidation, he resigned, believing his departure might shield the organization from further fallout. Leadership passed to Dale McElwee and later to a VA social worker named Pat, as GLAD continued its cautious navigation between service provision and survival.

Internal strain intensified by 1988. Mical would later recall open confrontations at meetings as Chuck pressed the organization toward stronger advocacy and public accountability. Tensions sharpened when NO/AIDS warned that grant funds must be used strictly for education and support services, not political action. By the end of the decade, these differences were no longer private. They were structural fault lines.

By December 1989, the fault line between GLAD and ACT UP Shreveport had moved from private frustration to public rupture. GLAD had emerged as an education and prevention oriented organization, dependent on state funding and navigating instability under mounting scrutiny. Chuck had attempted to work within GLAD, pressing for stronger advocacy and direct engagement with institutional failures, but reform from the inside proved limited.

At a December board meeting that framed AIDS primarily as an educational issue, ACT UP members challenged the organization's reluctance to confront LSU Medical Center and its unwillingness to demand participation in emerging AIDS drug trials. The exchange grew tense and ended with ACT UP members being removed—an early clash that made clear the divide between caution and confrontation.

The divide was strategic. GLAD operated cautiously within a fragile funding landscape. ACT UP insisted on confrontation. December 1989 made that divide unmistakable and clarified ACT UP Shreveport's identity: urgency over caution, confrontation over accommodation.

Urgency shifted from dispute to demand. In December 1989, ACT UP Shreveport confronted LSU Medical Center directly. What began as a formal complaint, including a December 8 letter to Dean Dr. Darryl Williams, became a nearly four-hour meeting with the dean, Dr. John King of infectious diseases, and other department leaders.

Activists arrived with documentation and national research, pressing LSU on its refusal to participate in AIDS drug trials and questioning the absence of coordinated local research for patients in Shreveport. They challenged reporting practices, demanded transparency about funding and infrastructure, and insisted that local patients deserved equal access to emerging therapies.

Dr. Williams cautioned that agitation risked polarization. ACT UP members countered that urgency required confrontation. The meeting marked the beginning of a sustained and increasingly public conflict between ACT UP Shreveport and the region's most powerful medical institution.

In January 1990, *The Shreveport Journal* weighed in with an editorial titled "Act Smart," praising GLAD's educational focus while warning that ACT UP's tactics risked alienating public support. The editorial urged activism that was orderly and cooperative rather than confrontational. ACT UP had already chosen a different path.

The actions did not unfold one at a time or in neat containment. They overlapped, accelerated, and collided—each building on the last until what might have been isolated confrontations became a pattern, then a presence the city could no longer absorb quietly.

The reckoning did not remain confined to boardrooms. That same month, ACT UP Shreveport confronted workplace discrimination after Vern Ransburg Jr., a cook at the Pickle Barrel restaurant, was fired when the owners learned he was HIV-positive. Vern, born February 19, 1963, would die later that year, on October 6, 1990.

According to Robert Darrow's oral history, the group responded with a sit-in, occupying a large table in the center of the small restaurant. Members ordered only water and refused to leave, effectively shutting the business down until management agreed to engage. Staff returned to the table repeatedly, asking whether anyone was ready to order, and each time the answer was the same: "Water, please." There was no bill, no movement, no resolution. Around them, other customers were seated, drinks arrived, food was served, and the ACT UP table did not move. It became impossible not to notice that something was happening. Alana Oldham, Chuck Selber, Richard Kightlinger, Robert Darrow, Judy Blue, Buddy Williamson, Deborah Allen, Bruce Young, and Joe DeSantis were among those present.

Richard later dated the action to January 1990 based on his appearance at the time, recalling that he had grown a beard after relinquishing his Miss Monte's My Way crown and that Bruce Young, an early ACT UP Shreveport member, became ill shortly afterward. The action drew local media coverage and forced public attention onto HIV discrimination in Shreveport.

By February 1990, confrontation moved from exposure to structural demand. At a Northwest Louisiana AIDS Task Force meeting, Chuck and Robert, representing ACT UP Shreveport, challenged the absence of a person living with AIDS on the board of directors, insisting that those most affected must have a voice in decisions shaping care, funding, and policy. When officials responded with assurances about past representation and the need to protect confidentiality, the activists made clear that symbolic inclusion was not enough. Their demand was direct.

Under sustained pressure, the Task Force relented and appointed several people living with AIDS, including Chuck and Robert. The insistence aligned with a growing federal mandate that people living with AIDS be formally represented in planning bodies receiving Ryan White funds. What began as a challenge in a meeting room in Shreveport helped translate urgency into structural requirement.

Confrontation next turned toward the city's gatekeepers of narrative. In early 1990, ACT UP Shreveport entered the newsroom of *The Shreveport Times* and began "papering" it—placing protest flyers on every desk, across counters, along hallways—an image of an iceberg accusing the paper of reporting only the visible tip while the mass of suffering remained submerged. They pushed past the front desk and fanned out across the room until the newsroom itself became a stage. Chuck led from the front, Gary close behind, others moving with purpose.

"DO YOUR JOB!" they shouted, followed by the chant—"ACT UP! FIGHT BACK! FIGHT AIDS!"—again and again, until the clatter of typewriters thinned and stalled. Reporters stared. Some looked stunned, others visibly uneasy, the interruption so far outside the ordinary rhythm of the newsroom that it shattered concentration on the spot. A few were frustrated as much as startled, struggling to recover what they had been doing while the chant filled the room and then lingered after the activists left. The action was not sparked by a single article but by absence—by the paper's refusal to cover AIDS in any sustained way: no investigation into failing hospitals, no probing of local neglect, no reckoning with the city's mounting deaths.

The response from the newspaper was hostile, but the confrontation forced a conversation that silence had long deferred. In the aftermath, *The Shreveport Times* installed scanners, locked doors requiring security codes, and security gates—barriers that had not been there before.

If the press would not investigate, the physicians would be confronted directly. In March 1990, ACT UP Shreveport carried its precision into the old Shreveport Convention Center, where the Shreveport Medical Society was hosting a regional conference. Robert Darrow, Deborah Allen, Alana Oldham, Chad Cromer, and Kenny King slipped into the luncheon hall just before the physicians arrived, moving between round tables as servers set down salads. Assuming they were part of the event staff, no one stopped them.

On every seat and every plate, they placed the same flier used to paper the offices of *The Shreveport Times*—an indictment of how people with AIDS were being treated and the lack of urgency in research. There was no chanting, no storming of the room. They left the message waiting. Many of the doctors likely dismissed it at first as just another handout among many. But once seated among strangers and forced to look more closely, they were confronted with a message far harder to brush aside. When the doctors sat down, the confrontation was already in their hands.

The pressure did not ease. On April 2, 1990, at a 9:30 a.m. press conference at the Radisson Hotel in Shreveport, ACT UP Shreveport publicly demanded the resignation of Dr. Perry Rigsby, Chancellor of LSU Medical Center. Standing together—Chuck Selber, Deborah Allen, Joe DeSantis, Gewel White, Joey Celmer, Kurt Pickett, Kenny King, Bonnie Parker, and others—the group charged LSU with mistreatment of people with AIDS.

They cited the use of large "caution" and biohazard signs on patients' doors as stigmatizing, reports of nurses refusing to feed patients or respond to call buttons, and the hospital's refusal to participate in national AIDS drug trials that would have given local patients access to experimental treatments. They also accused administrators of rejecting research funding, failing to recruit key leadership, and offering only lip service when confronted.

Reading from a prepared statement, Chuck declared that "a distinct and direct message" must be delivered to the National Institutes of Health and funding agencies nationwide. The demand did not succeed—Rigsby responded the following day that he had no intention of stepping down and defended LSU's record—but April 1990 marked a turning point. ACT UP Shreveport had named LSU Medical Center as a central site of harm and made clear that it would not retreat.

Two weeks later, confrontation moved into sacred space. On April 14, 1990, during Shreveport's annual Holocaust Remembrance service at Broadmoor Baptist Church—a ceremony drawing nearly four hundred attendees—ACT UP intervened in a silence that had long gone unchallenged. Year after year, the litany of suffering named Jews, Romani, and the disabled, but not the homosexuals who had also been imprisoned and murdered under the pink triangle.

For Chuck, both Jewish and gay, that omission was personal. Alongside Bryan Sullivan, Joe DeSantis, Alana Oldham, Deborah Allen, Robert Darrow, Richard Kightlinger, Kenny King, and Gary Cathey, ACT UP members rose without a word. Each held a pink triangle placard—the badge once forced onto gay men in Nazi camps, now lifted in defiance. They did not chant. They did not interrupt. They stood shoulder to shoulder.

Bryan Sullivan would later recall the grief on Chuck's face as he raised his triangle, calling it one of the most courageous moments he had witnessed. They stood. And stood. And stood. Then they walked out, leaving behind a silence that could no longer be ignored.

By late summer, confrontation moved into the civic arena. On August 29, 1990, ACT UP Shreveport carried the AIDS crisis into a mayoral forum at LSUS. Joined by the University Program Council, the Gay and Lesbian Parent Network, and the Shreveport/Bossier Gay Political Alliance, ACT UP pressed seven candidates on policy, funding, police leadership, sex education, and the city's response to AIDS.

What began with general agreement that Shreveport must "get its house in order" fractured under pointed questions that exposed divisions and evasions. Some candidates affirmed the right of gay and

AIDS organizations to ask hard questions but hesitated when pressed on specifics. The sharpest exchanges centered on whether sexual orientation should affect public employment, particularly the position of police chief.

Jerry Jones and C.O. Simpkins drew applause for stating that job performance, not sexual orientation, should determine leadership. Others offered cautious responses that revealed how unprepared many were to address the crisis.

On November 19, 1990, ACT UP Shreveport transformed a touring production of *Hair* at the Shreveport Riverview Theatre into an AIDS protest. Planned in advance by Chuck in coordination with the road manager, the action began the moment the final chord sounded. From within the audience, ACT UP members—including Chuck, Alana Oldham, Kurt Pickett, Kenny King, and others—rose and began the chant: "ACT UP, FIGHT BACK, FIGHT AIDS!"

What began as voices in the seats swelled as the cast joined in, moving up the aisles and into the lobby. Theatergoers exiting the show were met with banners and leaflets. Alana Oldham, an ACT UP Shreveport member who would become one of the group's most consistent organizers, later recalled the exhilaration of watching the rebellion of *Hair* spill offstage into Shreveport and the camaraderie that followed as activists and actors gathered afterward. In later years, some would claim the protest never happened. But it did. It was covered in *The Shreveport Times*, preserving in print the night a musical about protest became one.

On December 1, 1990, ACT UP Shreveport marked Day Without Art at the Turner Art Center as part of the national observance launched by Visual AIDS to coincide with World AIDS Day. It was the first time the two were observed together locally, linking Shreveport to a growing national ritual of mourning and protest.

In Shreveport, Kurt Pickett, Robert Darrow, Kenny King, and Deborah Allen joined artists Bill Lindsey, Jon Breedlove, and Michael Moore. Activists cut black plastic trash bags and covered artwork at several museums, turning gallery walls into fields of absence. Bryan Sullivan described it as an international gesture of mourning. Bruce Allen, Centenary College of Louisiana's art department chair, helped shroud the pieces, and Deborah and Mary "Cat Food Mary" Sparkman documented the action on film.

The city initially supported the effort and assisted in covering the artwork, though that cooperation would not last.

In April 1991, ACT UP Shreveport picked a new wall. On a Saturday night, members spray-painted the side of St. Joseph's Catholic Church on Patton Avenue with a phrase widely attributed to Gloria Steinem: "If men could get pregnant, abortion would be a sacrament." Parishioners arrived for Sunday Mass and saw it in daylight.

The choice of site was symbolic rather than personal. Monsignor Murray Clayton, who later passed away on September 25, 2015, had supported local queer organizations and was not publicly hostile toward the community. The target was the broader authority of the Catholic Church, whose opposition to abortion and reproductive autonomy shaped law and policy far beyond Shreveport.

That spring, confrontation took on a different register. As David Duke campaigned for governor of Louisiana, ACT UP Shreveport faced a threat rooted in political power. Duke, a former Grand Dragon of the Ku Klux Klan, was not a fringe candidate in North Louisiana; he was winning votes. Gary Cathey later recalled that in many northern parishes, Duke carried elections outright.

When Duke scheduled a rally at the Community Center in Minden, Gary Cathey and Bryan Sullivan set out with protest signs, expecting others to oppose him. Instead, they found no demonstrators. The crowd inside was filled with familiar faces—neighbors, classmates, people they had grown up with—cheering Duke on.

Confronted with that reality, they paused. Raising signs in that room would not have sparked dialogue; it could have sparked violence. They left the signs behind and walked in anyway, choosing presence over spectacle.

The lesson did not fade. It resurfaced two years later, in August 1993, when the Knights of the Ku Klux Klan rallied on the steps of the Caddo Parish Courthouse—white shirts marked with cross insignias, Confederate symbols visible—ACT UP Shreveport placed itself in the frame. Newspaper accounts described a modest crowd, heavy police presence, and Klansmen speaking beneath mounted deputies while denying ties to violence.

Just beyond the police tape, near the courthouse statue, Micah Harold, Kurt Pickett, James Smith, Deborah Allen, Lynn Pyle, Brandon Pyle, and others stood in protest. In a defiant kiss-in, Kurt kissed Jerry Brown, a friend, in full view of Klansmen and television cameras. Deborah later recalled that the gesture nearly sparked a riot as Klansmen surged forward before police intervened.

Buddy Williamson, photographing the scene, described it as feeling "like stepping back 100 years," the air thick with shouts about the rebel flag while two men calmly claimed their right to love. Local broadcasts carried images of robed white supremacy alongside queer defiance on the courthouse steps.

In June 1991, at a corner table inside Shoney's—the same place where ACT UP Shreveport gathered to plan, argue, and organize—protest began with a marker and a stack of dollar bills. Micah Harold, Deborah Allen, Robert Darrow, Kenny King, Michael Moore, and others wrote "Queer Money" or "Queer $$" across hundreds of one-dollar bills before sending them back into circulation.

At a time when queer people were dying of AIDS while paying taxes to a government slow to respond, the marked bills carried a message: we are not invisible. Each transaction became a quiet confrontation.

Days later, that insistence returned to GLAD itself. ACT UP again pressed the organization publicly, challenging what it saw as caution without advocacy and forcing a confrontation that had already been building. The divide between service and direct action was no longer theoretical—it was visible.

By autumn, the argument moved from philosophy to funding. On October 9, 1991, ACT UP Shreveport stepped into a Region 7 AIDS Consortium meeting, part of the Louisiana Department of Health and Hospitals (DHH), and confronted how Ryan White CARE Act dollars were being allocated across Northwest Louisiana.

The Region 7 HIV Planning Coalition, chaired by Patsy McGee of the Office of Public Health and later formalized as the Ryan White Consortium, brought together hospitals, home health agencies, and service providers competing for contracts. Patients were there too. Robert Darrow, Deborah Allen, Paul Weiss, and other ACT UP members took seats alongside administrators, insisting that people living with AIDS be more than statistics on a grant application.

Robert later recalled that "anybody who could make a dime off of us was at these meetings," yet ACT UP refused to relinquish that space. They pressed for transparency and equitable distribution so Shreveport–Bossier patients would not be left behind.

In September 1992, during the week of the outing, several ACT UP Shreveport members pushed confrontation beyond meetings and into the streets. Gary Cathey and Justin Normand conceived a flier that left little to interpretation. They clipped Congressman Jim McCrery's photograph from a newspaper and paired it with a graphic image of an erect penis, positioning his face so that he appeared to be looking up at it in a way that suggested a sexual act.

The design was intentionally crude, assembled by hand by Justin Normand and Gary Cathey at a late-night Kinko's in Dallas before being reproduced in several dozen copies. They worked quickly, finishing the layout before leaving the city after 11 p.m., carrying the copies with them to Shreveport.

That weekend, after returning from Dallas, Justin Normand and Gary Cathey picked up a carload of ACT UP members and moved through Shreveport and Bossier, stapling and gluing the flyers to telephone poles, storefronts, restaurant restrooms, and even the monument sign outside McCrery's congressional office on Youree Drive.

The station wagon carried Kenny King, Kurt Pickett, Buddy Williamson, Gary Cathey, Justin Normand, and Brandy Roberts as they circled the city that night. The image was graphic—intentionally so. Where the outing exposed hypocrisy in words, the flier answered in pictures.

Not every action moved through a formal vote or scheduled meeting. This one grew from the outrage surrounding the outing.

By early 1993, accountability returned to the street. In February, ACT UP Shreveport confronted what it saw as AIDS profiteering by Capri, Shapes, and Ultimate Appearances—three businesses that had promoted a December 1992 fashion and hair show as an "AIDS benefit." Advertised locally and promising proceeds to organizations providing direct care and risk-reduction services, the event had generated publicity but not payment.

Months later, the promised funds had not arrived. According to Deborah Allen, repeated phone calls and letters went unanswered. On the night of the protest, Deborah and Kurt Pickett stood outside and turned the unanswered question into a public challenge: "Where is the money?" Flyers named the owners, accused them of exploiting the crisis, and called for a boycott.

Media coverage amplified the protest. Attendance suffered. Under mounting pressure, some funds were eventually directed to the Philadelphia Center.

On April 17, 1993, ACT UP Shreveport returned to LSU Medical

Center, confronting the hospital's use of bright yellow "universal precautions" signs placed on the doors of patients with blood-borne infections—signs activists argued appeared almost exclusively on the rooms of those living with HIV. At a press conference outside the hospital, Kurt Pickett, Deborah Allen, Ed Brooks, and Joey Celmer denounced the practice, insisting that while the notices did not name a diagnosis, their color and placement marked AIDS patients as dangerous.

Kurt warned that the signs created the illusion that precautions were necessary only where a "big yellow flag" appeared, undermining the meaning of universal precautions. Hospital officials maintained the signs were standard infection-control measures used for multiple diseases, and Marc acknowledged the medical rationale while urging consistency: either remove the signs or place them on every patient's door. Other local hospitals confirmed they relied on internal policy rather than visible warnings.

For ACT UP, the issue was not gloves or handwashing protocols. The signs turned safety language into a public badge of contagion.

Weeks later, confrontation moved from hospital corridors to city streets. In May 1993, ACT UP Shreveport answered institutional silence with satire. After repeated attempts by same-sex couples to report domestic violence were dismissed by the Shreveport Police Department—complaints treated as illegible because they did not fit a husband-and-wife script—Kenny King, with the assistance of Kurt Pickett and Bryan Sullivan, designed a full page mint-green flyer featuring a drawing of "Madge," the Palmolive manicurist, alongside the line, "QUEERNESS, YOU'RE SOAKING IN IT." The entire campaign was a pointed satire of the long-running Palmolive commercials, repurposing their familiar cadence to expose the absurdity of a system that refused to recognize queer relationships as real, let alone worthy of protection.

Kenny King, Bryan Sullivan, Kurt Pickett, Richard Williams, James Smith, Alan Bowers, and Robbie Smith stapled the flyers across Highland, placing them at the same height along telephone poles and storefronts, forming a continuous visual line. There was no press conference, no permit, no coverage. Within days, police were seen tearing the sheets down.

But the point had already been made.

In late April 1993, Shreveport police began investigating the death of Frank *LaFayette*, a fifty-year-old man found bludgeoned in a downtown alley. Activists described the attack as brutal and anti-gay in tone, but authorities hesitated to label it a hate crime. Newspaper coverage debated language while neighbors debated blame.

For those who had watched violence against gay men minimized for years, the argument over terminology felt like evasion. A man was dead. The city argued over definitions.

Working from Kenny's apartment, they compiled a list of confirmed attack sites through trusted allies who tracked what the press and police did not. Kenny cut stencils that read "**A GAY MAN WAS MURDERED HERE!**", and the small group—Kenny King, Kurt Pickett, and Jerry Smith—set out with spray paint in hand.

They chose bright colors that refused erasure and marked sidewalks and parking lots where violence had occurred, including Clyde Fant Parkway's Hamels Park, a known gay cruising area, where a man had been killed and no hate crime was reported. They moved quickly and silently, leaving the message in seven or eight places before the city fully woke.

By dawn, Shreveport had been mapped in neon grief.

The conflict did not end in 1993. On December 1, 1995—World AIDS Day—ACT UP Shreveport closed the Texas Street Bridge after city officials and the Shreveport Regional Arts Council refused to turn off the bridge's neon lights for A Day Without Art. The brightly lit span, promoted as one of the city's most visible public art projects, stood in contrast to galleries across the country that went dark to mark the cultural toll of AIDS.

For activists, the glow felt like denial.

Kurt Pickett, Kenny King, Buddy Williamson, Deborah Allen, Don Mathis, and others stretched rope around the bridge's pylons and across its lanes, blocking traffic on both ends around 8:45 p.m. red biohazard bags were strung across the roadway as cars halted and news cameras arrived. Drivers slowed in confusion, unsure whether the blockade was official or improvised, scanning for some sign of city authority that never came. For the activists, the moment shifted quickly from plan to consequence, the questions becoming real almost at once: when would police arrive, and what would happen when they did?

The staging was deliberate. Kenny, an artist by instinct, understood the power of image—the rope cutting the span, the red bags flashing against the neon glow. The blockade was brief but unmistakable.

"That is the biggest piece of art in this city," Don Mathis, an ACT UP

Shreveport member and prevention coordinator with the Philadelphia Center, told reporters. "That is a travesty in that we need leadership to end this disease."

At 9:10 p.m., the mayor ordered the lights turned off, but activists said it was not enough.

For years they had demanded attention—now they stopped traffic on the city's central artery. The bridge went dark as the river moved beneath it, and the silence that followed felt different, not empty but charged with what had already been forced into view.

By then, confrontation had taken on many forms—loud and quiet, public and unannounced. It surfaced in hospital rooms, in meeting halls, and in streets where people refused to move, shifting shape but not intent. What bound it was not method, but insistence. And after the chants faded and the streets cleared, that resistance did not disappear. It remained—defiant, unannounced, and just as deliberate—arriving without noise at all.

In February 1991, a different kind of confrontation arrived—one stitched instead of shouted. Local organizers brought the NAMES Project AIDS Memorial Quilt to Bossier City, the first attempt to assemble Ark-La-Tex memorial quilt panels outside of Baton Rouge or New Orleans. Spearheaded by Chris Free and supported by Chuck Selber, Richard Kightlinger, Gary Cathey, Justin Normand, and others, the ten-person host committee framed the display not simply as memorial but as reckoning.

Louisiana had already recorded more than 2,200 AIDS cases, including over 100 in Caddo Parish. When approximately 800 quilt panels arrived at the Bossier Civic Center that July, covering nearly 20,000 square feet, statistics dissolved into fabric. Each 3-by-6-foot panel carried a name, a photograph, a scrap of denim or lace, a fragment of handwriting.

Community leaders read hundreds of names aloud. By design, there was no music—only the steady cadence of names spoken into the open air, each one carrying its own weight, its own unfinished story. Interpreters provided by the Betty and Leonard Phillips Deaf Action Center translated the ceremony into American Sign Language, ensuring every name was seen as well as heard. With special permission from the Names Project, The Sign Company performed *That's What Friends Are For* in ASL, transforming the song into movement—hands shaping grief and memory into air.

   DR. DAVID W. HYLAN

For the first time on that scale, Shreveport and Bossier were asked not to debate AIDS, but to stand before the dead and say their names. For some, the impact was immediate and overwhelming: sadness, emptiness, and a hollowing dread at the realization that this was what remained after sickness and loss, and that others would follow the same path from diagnosis to death to a quilt panel.

Two years later, the Quilt returned to Shreveport during Centenary College's AIDS Education and Awareness Week, unfolding across the small stage of the Hargrove Memorial Amphitheater. The space was tight, and arranging the panels required careful maneuvering so visitors could move without stepping on memory.

Susan "Susie" McClamroch coordinated the display, joined by Gary Cathey, Justin Normand, Judy Blue, and Flo Selber. Justin transported panels from Dallas; together they lifted, aligned, and shifted fabric inch by inch, creating narrow pathways so visitors could stand before the names.

Susie had stitched many of the local panels herself, channeling grief into thread and holding close the stories of men the community had known. After the exhibition closed, Gary and Justin carried her panels back to Dallas to be formally accepted into the national NAMES Project, ensuring they became part of the larger tapestry of remembrance.

In November 1997, the Quilt traveled into more reluctant territory. Gary Cathey and his husband Justin Normand organized a display in Minden, Louisiana, a town that had often preferred abstraction to acknowledgment.

The rollout began before the Civic Center opened. A banner stretched across the entrance to downtown, and inside the Webster Parish Public Library, Gary and Justin installed a display of AIDS information, images, and brochures placed where visitors could not avoid them. The materials remained in place for the week leading up to the event. *The Shreveport Times* ran coverage, and one Minden resident asked the question that hung in the air: "What does AIDS have to do with Minden?"

The answer waited at the Minden Civic Center. When the Quilt was unfolded there, panels lay side by side, celebrity and neighbor collapsed into the same cloth. Rock Hudson rested beside sons of Webster Parish. Outside, red ribbons were fastened to each City Hall column. Coca-Cola of Minden sponsored the banner as a public gesture of support.

Chuck's panel drew people close. His niece Jill Selber Handaly had asked each of the nieces and nephews to draw their favorite memories of Uncle Chuck, then stitched those drawings into the fabric, layering childhood color over adult grief. It was not only a memorial. It was a family album in cloth.

Once the panels were down on the Civic Center floor, the question from the newspaper stopped being rhetorical.

More than a decade later, on World AIDS Day, December 1, 2014, the Quilt appeared again, this time to the Municipal Auditorium in a different form. The panels did not lie flat across the floor. Most descended from the ceiling and the arena's first balcony railing in long vertical drops, so visitors walked among them looking up rather than down.

A few rested on tables and along the stage, but the dominant experience was upward—names suspended in air. More than a thousand people in Caddo Parish were living with HIV or AIDS, and statewide numbers remained above zero. "There's no good number above zero," said Eric Evans of the Philadelphia Center, which hosted the observance.

Through a grant from the Elton John AIDS Foundation, panels were secured through the NAMES Project's lending program. ACT UP Shreveport members worked alongside Philadelphia Center staff to measure, suspend, and arrange them across the auditorium's curved interior. Among those honored were Gewel White, Chris Free, Joe DeSantis, Vern Ransburg, Johnny Benson, and Chuck Selber.

The quilt filled the room, wrapping partway around the hall. What had once forced the city to see now asked it to remember.

But memory was never the end of the fight. The forces shaping those losses extended beyond Shreveport, beyond any single room or gathering. To confront them would require reaching outward—building connections and stepping into something larger through state and national collaborations.

CHAPTER 5
STATE AND NATIONAL COLLABORATIONS

*"It was shocking to me, coming from Shreveport, Louisiana, to realize that
our little group was part of something so big."*
>—Alana Oldham, ACT UP Shreveport member

The conversations that once fit inside Shreveport's living rooms had
outgrown them, spilling into borrowed spaces and louder gatherings. For
months, casseroles, coffee, and anger had been enough. But ACT UP
Shreveport soon looked outward and saw their struggle reflected beyond
Shreveport. They carried their grief into apartments and quieter corners.
News from New York and San Francisco did not surprise them—it
confirmed what they already knew: the silence was national, deliberate,
and deadly. Budgets were not simply numbers on a page. They were
carved up by congressional horse-trading long before NIH bureaucrats
divided the money, determining who might have a chance to live and
who would be left behind.

By 1990, they were ready to take that risk. ACT UP Shreveport
was still young, rough around the edges, but its members felt the pull to
stand shoulder to shoulder with thousands. When the call came, Alana
Oldham later described the shock of it—the realization that a handful
of people from Shreveport had stepped onto a stage that stretched across
the nation.

The call came for a massive demonstration at the National Institutes of Health in Bethesda, Maryland, on May 21, 1990. National ACT UP was organizing a die-in to protest the slow pace of clinical trials and the federal government's reluctance to release promising AIDS drugs. From Shreveport, five said yes: Gary Cathey, Robert Darrow, Joe DeSantis, Alana Oldham, and Chuck Selber. Their decision would carry Shreveport's name onto the national stage.

The logistics were daunting. Plane tickets had to be purchased, banners prepared, talking points memorized. Chuck and Robert pressed for the group to be as visible as possible, knowing that even small numbers could carry weight if they marched under their own banner. Gary was nervous—travel meant exposure; his face might appear in newspapers back home—but he agreed. "It was scary," he admitted, "but we knew we couldn't sit it out."

When they arrived in Washington, the scale overwhelmed them. The night before the protest, hundreds gathered in a church. It was not crowded so much as charged, carrying the sense of organized chaos waiting to break loose the next day. Each ACT UP chapter stood and announced where it was from, and when ACT UP Shreveport rose, the room answered with applause and cheers. Gary later understood that response as recognition that Shreveport represented small-town America, proof that the movement had reached even into the Bible Belt. For the Shreveport group, the feeling was exhilarating, not unlike a first Pride, the sudden certainty that they were not alone and never had been. In that church, they were part of something larger, moving in the same direction.

Robert Darrow found himself sitting next to Jeanne White, Ryan White's mother. The Indiana teenager had become the face of pediatric AIDS after being barred from his middle school, and his death in April 1990 had shattered hearts across America. "I remember sitting there, side by side with her, holding her hand," Robert said. "It struck me then—this epidemic was never only about gay men. It was about families, mothers and sons, fathers and daughters, all caught in the crossfire of fear and ignorance."

The next day, over one thousand activists converged on the NIH campus. Protesters carried banners, staged skits and dances, and finally lay down in the grass and across the road for a massive die-in. Uniformed officers and mounted police ringed the lawn, but six hundred bodies pressed into the ground made their point without violence—the weight

　　　　　　　　DR. DAVID W. HYLAN

of those bodies spelling out lives abandoned. Nothing about it felt distant. Protesters saw an unending crowd of signs, bodies, and police. They heard chants, whistles, and a constant swell of voices rising against the NIH buildings. Smoke bombs bled color into the air. Grass, pavement, sweat, and the heat of other bodies made the action physical in every sense. Organizers passed water bottles hand to hand, and linked arms turned the protest into something not only seen, but felt.

Smoke bombs drifted through the crowd in bursts of color—pink, purple, yellow—rising in defiance. Robert said they filled the air like fireworks, with pink rising above the rest. "Many of them had to be pink, of course," he added, a flash of gallows humor in a day heavy with grief and anger.

Later, Gary explained how surreal it felt: "There we were, from Shreveport of all places, carrying this plain black-and-white banner with our chapter's name on it. As protesters gathered, the organizers pulled us from the crowd and placed us in the front. They wanted the media to see that AIDS was affecting the heartland of America, not only the big cities. And suddenly our banner led people onto the NIH campus—thousands behind us. Gary later explained how surreal it felt: "There we were ... And suddenly our banner led people onto the NIH campus—thousands behind us. I thought: how in the world did I get here?" The moment the organizers moved ACT UP Shreveport to the front, it all became real. They were no longer simply joining the protest. They were leading it, the first faces the NIH would see through its windows. Backs straightened. Shoulders went back. Heads lifted. Pride moved through the group as tangibly as fear. Alana added with a laugh that from the cameras' angle it looked as though ACT UP Shreveport was an army of thousands, when in truth they were only a handful of people. Robert was interviewed that day and later featured in a Washington Post article, "The Preacher's Son," highlighting the diversity of those affected by AIDS.

The coverage reached home quickly. *The Shreveport Journal* ran "5 AIDS group members return from D.C. march," listing the Shreveport delegation by name and noting that arrests were made—none local. Chuck Selber told the paper the protest was about more than theater: "AIDS research is underfunded." At the same time, CNN's thirty-minute news loop aired NIH footage for two days, with the ACT UP Shreveport banner visible at the forefront. In a city where AIDS coverage often amounted to whispers, those images—and those names—landed hard at home.

On the campus, NIH officials acknowledged the protesters' frustration. Dr. Anthony Fauci admitted he sympathized with their anger but warned against "gross distortions of reality," insisting progress against HIV had been unprecedented. NIH acting director William Raub offered a measured response: the institute was "driven by compassion and commitment," he said, while applauding police for keeping order. With AZT still the only federally approved drug, protesters countered with chants that echoed across the buildings: "TEN YEARS, A BILLION DOLLARS, ONE DRUG, BIG DEAL." "THIS IS NOT A COFFEE BREAK—THIS IS THE AIDS CRISIS." "WE'RE HERE! WE'RE QUEER!" At times, the chant shifted—"AND SO ARE SOME OF YOU." A sharper edge that unsettled the crowd.

Later, Alana said she never forgot the scale: "In Shreveport we were twenty, maybe thirty people crammed together. But here—here it was a thousand plus. And to think our banner was at the front of the march onto the NIH campus. It made me feel like we weren't alone anymore."

They lobbied Louisiana senators and representatives while in Washington, pressing for more research dollars. Most offices offered polite nods and platitudes, but the message landed: Shreveport wasn't silent, and its activists weren't content to fight only at home.

When they flew back to Louisiana, their bodies were heavy with fatigue and the day's chants still rang in their ears. Beneath the weariness was exhilaration. In their luggage they carried more than protest flyers; they carried the certainty that their chapter was part of something larger.

The trip had changed them. Seeing thousands converge at the National Institutes of Health made clear that the struggle was not only in the hospital wards or the streets—it was inside the agencies whose definitions and budgets decided lives. Bureaucracy had become a battlefield. That understanding followed them home, shaping every action that came after. The next test would come not in Washington, but in Louisiana.

On June 25, 1990, that test came when ACT UP Shreveport crossed parish lines and joined ACT UP New Orleans in one of the largest acts of AIDS civil disobedience the Deep South had seen. The target was Charity Hospital's C-100 Clinic, the state's primary HIV outpatient and experimental drug-trial site, whose funding had been slashed from $3.3 million to $1.4 million even as patients waited as long as five months for appointments. Chuck Selber made clear beforehand that this would not be symbolic. "Civil disobedience works," he said, invoking the Boston Tea Party and promising arrests if lawmakers refused to restore funding.

On a humid afternoon along Loyola Avenue, activists moved from speeches to action, sitting in rows across rush-hour traffic outside the State Office Building and near Charity Hospital, blocking the street in deliberate defiance. Nearly fifty protesters went limp as police lifted them one by one into a waiting bus, their chants of "ACT UP! FIGHT BACK! FIGHT AIDS!" echoing over the bullhorn warnings. Among those arrested were Chuck and Alana Oldham, and two-thirds of those taken into custody were from Shreveport, not New Orleans.

Organized with logistical support from the NO/AIDS Task Force and local leaders, and amplified by television cameras and front-page coverage, the action forced Louisiana's funding cuts into public view. It also exposed another layer of the struggle: debates over whether publicly labeling HIV clinics endangered patients in a climate of stigma and fear. June 1990 revealed something essential about ACT UP in Northwest Louisiana. It was no longer confined to city limits or willing to rely on polite appeals while lives were placed on hold.

By late September 1990, ACT UP Shreveport brought the national Miller Beer boycott to the doorstep of Thrifty Liquor on Youree Drive, turning an ordinary Friday retail rush into a pointed act of resistance. Charlsa Henderson, Camille LeGrand, Alana Oldham, and Shelly Bass, among others, stood at the center of the protest, joining a nationwide campaign targeting Miller Beer and Marlboro cigarettes, both produced by Philip Morris, whose political contributions helped keep Senator Jesse Helms in power. To activists, Helms embodied institutional contempt— railing against gay men, obstructing AIDS funding, and casting blame on the communities most devastated by the epidemic.

Supporting Miller, they argued, meant subsidizing that hostility. Outside the store, picket signs and chants reframed the act of purchasing beer as a moral choice; protesters promoted Budweiser and handed out free beer to underscore that consumer dollars carried consequence. The chant "Queer $$" circulated through the demonstration, a reminder that queer spending power could be mobilized. In Shreveport, as in cities across the country, the boycott made clear that silence would no longer be subsidized, and corporate complicity in homophobia would be met with organized resistance. But boycotts alone could not change the definitions that determined who lived and who did not.

The year closed in Atlanta. On December 3, 1990, ACT UP Shreveport joined hundreds of activists at the Centers for Disease Control headquarters, where, before they set foot on campus, Chuck Selber had already pried open one door. After months of letters and arguments, he convinced the agency to replace "homosexual contact" with "male-to-male sexual contact"—a technical shift that kept men who did not identify as gay from vanishing in the statistics. Technical, yes—but in those numbers lived truth and survival.

The road there was long, and they rented a Winnebago that, as Robert put it, was "the biggest damn thing I'd ever driven." It swayed like a ship in a storm. Dishes rattled in the cabinets, nerves in the back seats. The space was cramped. Everyone had a seat, but no one could spread out, and a faint smell of exhaust lingered beneath the stale air of the road. Among the Shreveport crew was Kenny King—new to activism, still finding his footing—who also took a turn at the wheel as they pushed through the miles to Atlanta. Inside that lumbering vehicle, the mission moved with them. Everyone had something to say, and even when voices did not overlap, the weight of the trip filled the space. They were driving straight toward the agency that controlled definitions, funding, and the arithmetic of who counted as having AIDS—and who didn't.

By the time they reached Atlanta, rain slicked the pavement outside the CDC, turning protest signs to pulp and voices to determination. The crowd swelled into the hundreds, chanting against policies that wrote women out of the epidemic. Their signs said what the agency would not: "Women don't get AIDS—they just die from it." The phrase cut through the drizzle, exposing the bureaucratic blindness that had kept women off the CDC's official definition for years. Within the Shreveport contingent, Kenny King focused on that blindness—the flawed case definitions and reporting metrics that made the epidemic appear smaller than it was, erasing women and people of color from the record. Inside the Winnebago, they had joked about the chaos to come, but standing there in the rain, the joking gave way to rage.

It wasn't just the Shreveport regulars who stood in that rain. Five more joined from Natchitoches—among them Dave Herrell, a steady regional organizer, and Jason "J" Bratlie, a younger activist drawn to ACT UP's national confrontations. From Shreveport's side, Kenny King was in the line as well—fresh to ACT UP's national actions after jumping in at home, present more for duty than profile. Dave was young, new to activism, pulled in by friendship and urgency. "I didn't even know exactly what to expect," he said later, "but I knew I needed to be there." Jason was straight but resolute in his loyalty. He believed silence was complicity and refused to stand back while people he loved were being erased. During the protest, Jason spotted one of the fallen letters from the CDC sign on the ground. He picked up the letter F and kept it—a fragment of the moment, something he carried with him afterward.

The Winnebago became their rolling headquarters—part nervous laughter, part strategy session. Robert carried plastic file boxes crammed with research and clippings, determined that even on the road they would have the facts in hand. Jason cracked jokes to ease the tension, Dave sat quietly taking it all in, and Alana reminded them that what they were doing mattered, steadying nerves when the silence grew heavy. Every mile felt like both escape and exposure.

When they stepped out at the CDC, they carried the same black-and-white vinyl banner that had led the NIH march. Nothing flashy, nothing ornamental—just stark lettering: ACT UP AIDS Coalition to Unleash Power Shreveport, flanked on either end by the ACT UP logo, pink triangles cutting through the monochrome. At the CDC, it did not lead the protest as it had at NIH, but it was still raised above the crowd, a quiet declaration that a chapter from Shreveport had arrived.

The storm did not scatter the crowd. It sharpened their defiance. The rain meant nothing. If anything, it proved they were serious enough to do this under miserable conditions. Clothes were soaked to the point of uselessness. Paper signs bled ink and began to disintegrate. The cold settled in, but the volume never dropped. Protesters chained themselves to the CDC's glass-front headquarters, clothes plastered to their skin, voices rising through the downpour. Police and federal officials moved in with bolt cutters, snapping the chains one by one, but the sound only fed the chants. To the cameras, drenched activists refused to move, refused to be silent, even as the rain poured and the steel gave way. Shreveport's black-and-white banner, marked with a pink triangle and the Silence=Death symbol, was there in the crush—impossible to miss. Arrests mounted, but the Shreveport group was spared.

A few members of ACT UP Shreveport joined in unfurling a massive black banner draped across the CDC headquarters. Its message was blunt, painted in white letters against the wet stone: "CDC Kills." The cloth clung to the facade, a statement meant to be seen, not to last. The action carried ACT UP's mix of fury and theater—hundreds surrounding the glass-front headquarters, chanting, blocking entrances, staging die-ins. Shreveport's contingent pressed forward with their banner, part of the wave that forced cameras and microphones to capture what officials wanted to ignore. By then, the images were already on the nation's evening news.

Robert felt the weight of those hours. At the CDC, he understood the stakes. The definitions determined who was eligible for clinical drug trials and who received treatment. For ACT UP Shreveport, that was not theoretical. Back home, they knew HIV-positive women who were denied care because the CDC would not even allow them to be counted properly. Women were dying, yet the government insisted they didn't even have AIDS. This was not abstract policy—it was life and death. When word came later that the definition would change, the shift felt empowering, proof that pressure had reached the place where it mattered.

It was not only about visibility—it was about justice. The CDC's definition of AIDS excluded illnesses ravaging women, intravenous drug users, and people of color, reducing lives to categories that failed to capture the reality of the epidemic. The definition was more than semantics—it was the key to treatment, insurance, and survival. Standing in the rain, that knowledge settled in and did not leave.

Inside the chaos, Jason "J" Bratlie felt himself change. A straight man from Natchitoches, he had never imagined leading chants in the middle of a national protest. But surrounded by friends, carrying their banner, he realized allyship was not quiet support—it was standing in the same line of fire. "I wasn't scared for myself," he said later. "I was scared of what would happen if nobody did anything. So, I did."

Dave Herrell carried the memory of awe mixed with fear—the chants, the bodies in the street, the noise. "I thought, this is bigger than anything I've ever been part of," he said. "And I was proud—proud to say I came from Louisiana, proud to be standing there with them."

For hours, the protest locked the CDC in confrontation. Among the 1,100 activists who surrounded the building, the Shreveport delegation wasn't arrested that day—but they didn't need to be. Their banner endured, soaked and heavy, among chained and chanting bodies.

When the Winnebago rumbled back toward Louisiana, the exhaustion was bone-deep. Some dozed in the swaying bunks; others replayed the chants and confrontations in their minds. They stopped for gas station food, quick stretches at rest areas, coffee that never seemed strong enough. Inside that rattling behemoth was a new certainty: Shreveport had not only shown up—they had mattered.

When they returned, Shreveport looked unchanged—the same silence in its churches, the same hesitations in its newspapers, the same fears in its hospitals. ACT UP Shreveport was no longer the same.

They had marched at the NIH, shouted at the CDC, and carried their chapter's name in bold vinyl that turned heads. The fiercest battles still waited at home. Washington and Atlanta had given them momentum—but Shreveport would test whether that momentum could pierce the silence in its churches, its papers, and its politics.

Back in their living rooms and borrowed apartments, in Shoney's back rooms and casserole-strewn tables, one question trailed them: What comes next? The silence was not only in the streets and churches. It sat in the halls of power, even in Congress—where one of their own held the seat and turned away.

Even when they weren't boarding planes, ACT UP Shreveport stayed tied to the national movement. They carried out boycotts and actions in Shreveport, refusing Miller Beer and Marlboro cigarettes because of their connection to Jesse Helms—the senator who made cruelty into policy and turned AIDS into a weapon of stigma. They stood before the AIDS Memorial Quilt when it came south, touching the panels sewn in grief and adding the names of their own dead. On the first Day Without Art, they joined thousands across the country in recognizing vanished artists, with blank gallery walls echoing what had been stolen. At a Holocaust Remembrance service, they held up pink triangle placards in silence, tying their struggle to the memory of gay men imprisoned and murdered under another regime of erasure. On the steps of St. Joseph's, they spray-painted a demand for abortion rights, aligning with ACT UP's national fight for women's autonomy.

Each of these actions marked Shreveport as more than a provincial chapter. The national fight lived in north Louisiana—in its streets, its churches, and its bars. That refusal to remain quiet would turn inward, toward one of their own: a congressman who preached one thing and practiced another. Silence would not survive that confrontation.

Just weeks later, on September 22, 1992, when President George H. W. Bush arrived in Shreveport during the heat of campaign season, ACT UP Shreveport seized the moment. The protest was part of a coordinated national campaign challenging what activists saw as the administration's failure to treat AIDS as a national emergency, but in Northwest Louisiana the stakes were personal. Bush had publicly endorsed Congressman Jim McCrery, whose record had already made him a central adversary for local activists. A photograph in *The Shreveport Times* captured the confrontation: Kurt Pickett of ACT UP Shreveport arguing with a Bush supporter over the president's lack of support on AIDS, while Chad Cromer, an accomplished hairstylist, makeup artist, and ACT UP member, stood beside him holding a sign that read, "WHAT ABOUT AIDS?" The question cut through the campaign spectacle. September 1992 forced AIDS into proximity with presidential power on local ground, collapsing the illusion that Washington's indifference was distant. For ACT UP Shreveport, the White House was not an abstraction. Its politics landed squarely in the lives they were fighting to keep alive.

The following spring, in April 1993, ACT UP Shreveport joined the March on Washington for Lesbian, Gay and Bi Equal Rights and Liberation, sending forty-six local activists, including Robert, into what he described as a "sea of people" stretching from the base of Congress past the Washington Monument. Robert, speaking by mobile phone near Capitol Hill, said he felt he had "witnessed a part of history" and was grateful to have lived long enough to see it. While park officials estimated the crowd at 350,000, Robert believed nearly one million had gathered, a visible rebuke to any claim that gay Americans were marginal or silent. Marchers ranged from parents and veterans to political and religious groups and "Dykes on Bikes," their drums and chants echoing across the Washington Mall as entertainers performed nearby and a message of support from President Bill Clinton was read aloud. Even the presence of hostile signs along the route could not blunt the force of the day. April 1993 affirmed that Shreveport's activists were part of something national, demanding increased AIDS funding, an end to discrimination, and the right to live openly.

A month later, in May 1993, ACT UP Shreveport escalated its campaign against the failure of the C-100 Clinic at E.A. Conway Hospital (now University Health Conway) to open its long-promised AIDS clinic in Northeast Louisiana by turning disruption into a coordinated, multi-city effort. On May 27, ACT UP members across the nation attempted to tie up the telephone lines of Conway administrator Roy Bostick between 2 p.m. and 4 p.m. When callers were met only with "a click and a dial tone," Kurt Pickett welcomed it as confirmation the blitz was landing: "That's a good sign. Obviously, they got so many calls that they just got sick of it." Hospital officials later acknowledged that at least ten lines had been tied up.

The blitz targeted the hospital's continued delay in opening an AIDS clinic that had originally been set to open July 1, 1992. Members including Kurt Pickett, Deborah Allen, Gary Cathey, Don Mathis, and others organized a sweeping fax bomb and phone zap that reached far beyond a single machine. The Philadelphia Center's fax ran all day, but it was only one node in a wider network. Supporters used business offices, home lines, and out-of-state phones to flood Conway administrators with calls and transmissions protesting the hospital's continued practice of sending HIV patients 100 miles to Shreveport.

The tactic, drawn from national ACT UP strategy, was deliberately relentless: tying up lines, interrupting routine, and forcing administrators to confront a problem they had postponed. Conway officials insisted the hospital had received nearly $700,000 in AIDS funding over two years and claimed no separate clinic had ever been promised, arguing that patients would instead be treated within the hospital's regular clinics. The public defense only sharpened the activists' charge. The funding had been earmarked. Money had moved. Months had passed. HIV and AIDS patients were still waiting.

At the same time, activists carried their demands to Baton Rouge, accusing the Department of Health and Hospitals of mismanaging funds designated for the Monroe clinic and allowing the burden to fall on LSU Medical Center's already strained services. The Monroe phone and fax assault and the Baton Rouge protest were two parts of the same action: one jamming the hospital's lines, the other challenging state authority face-to-face. Patients were waiting months for care. ACT UP answered with noise and visibility, making it impossible for the state to pretend the problem was distant.

That same day, ACT UP Shreveport launched "Voodoo You," a theatrical, confrontational action aimed at both the Louisiana Department of Health and Hospitals and E.A. Conway Hospital in Monroe holding each accountable for a funding debacle that left people with HIV/AIDS traveling to LSU Medical Center in Shreveport for treatment even though Shreveport itself did not yet have a dedicated clinic.

Led by Deborah Allen, Kurt Pickett, Robert Darrow, James Smith, and Kenny King, activists stitched pink voodoo dolls, tucked written demands into plastic packets, and delivered them directly to administrators at DHH and at Conway, in some instances throwing the dolls into meetings while chanting "Voodoo You."

The symbolism was deliberate: not superstition, but satire sharpened into accusation, aimed at a system that had declared Conway out of compliance on May 10 for misusing more than $700,000 in HIV/AIDS funds, only to reverse its findings weeks later and claim no financial improprieties. ACT UP argued that less than $145,000 had gone toward actual HIV/AIDS services and that Monroe patients were still being diverted to Shreveport, creating strain and delay. Some officials tried to remain outwardly unmoved, unwilling to grant the action any visible power. Others seemed plainly affronted by what they regarded as unprofessional behavior. But by the time ACT UP left, the impression had been made. The dolls exposed what activists saw as bureaucratic neglect masked by paperwork.

Some insiders considered the action effective; others worried it risked alienating a conservative public. Media coverage was sparse. But the point had been made: when official language failed, ACT UP would invent its own.

Medical advances, including protease inhibitors, would soon begin to change the landscape. Combination therapies would soften some of the panic. But silence did not disappear. Funding battles returned. Political indifference resurfaced. When it did, ACT UP Shreveport answered again.

In February 2010, ACT UP Shreveport surfaced again when Governor Bobby Jindal came to speak at Summer Grove Baptist Church in south Shreveport, touting what he called the "Louisiana way" while defending his health care policies. For ACT UP members, the visit was urgent. Jindal's administration had created a waiting list for the AIDS Drug Assistance Program, leaving people living with HIV to wait for life-sustaining medications—a policy activists believed treated survival as expendable. The protest carried an old feeling in a newer moment, like being called back into formation. ACT UP knew this work. The instinct returned immediately.

Before the appearance, members gathered at the Philadelphia Center to print signs and prepare, then stood in the cold rain on the

     DR. DAVID W. HYLAN

public median outside the church entrance, careful not to trespass yet impossible to ignore. As worshippers exited the parking lot, some cursed, honked, and spat, their anger aimed at the small cluster holding signs that challenged the governor's record. What shocked the protesters was not political hostility but the source of it. They did not expect such open cruelty from people leaving church. Local media briefly covered the protest, airing interviews with both activists and Jindal, who dismissed them as "known radicals," but the segment was later pulled after pressure from his office.

The action rejected the claim that AIDS funding cuts were compassionate governance and insisted that policies made in Baton Rouge had consequences in Shreveport. February 2010 showed that even decades after the epidemic began, ACT UP was still willing to stand in the rain and interrupt political certainty with the reminder that lives were on the line.

But protest alone was never the whole strategy. It was only the visible edge of something deeper—the effort to name what others worked to obscure, to bring into view what had long been protected.

The real confrontation was not only in the streets, but in what was hidden—and what it meant to force it into the light through silence and exposure.

THE FACES OF RAGE

Before there were chapters, there were people.

These faces carried the weight long before the words tried to catch up. They argued, organized, comforted, buried their friends, and then got up the next morning to do it again. Some were loud. Some were quiet. None were untouched.

From nearly a thousand photographs, only a small portion remains here—fragments of lives caught in motion, in protest, in grief, in brief and fragile joy. What could be gathered has been carried forward.

What you see here is not arranged for narrative. It is not shaped for symmetry. It is what was captured in the middle of it—moments pulled from a time when survival itself felt uncertain. Look closely. The story has always belonged to them.

ACT UP MEMBERS

Debbie Allen	Jason Bratlie	Gary Cathey	C. Thad Coburn
Chad Cromer	Robert Darrow	Joe DeSantis	Chris Free
Micah Harold	Ashley Hazelton	Dave Herrell	Kenny King
Richard Kightlinger	Mark Anthony Lindsey	Tracy Murrell	Justin Normand

ACT UP MEMBERS

Alana Oldham

Kurt Pickett

Chuck Selber

James Smith

Bryan Sullivan

Judy Williams

Buddy Williamson

CHUCK SELBER'S FAMILY

Nancy Zeidman
Accado, Niece

Jill Selber Handaly,
Niece

Flo Selber,
Mother

Phyllis Selber,
Sister-in-Law

Sara Speer Selber,
Cousin

Leslie Zeidman
Snelgrove, Niece

Sandy Selber Sturm,
Niece

Jay Zeidman,
Nephew

Kay Zeidman,
Sister

Mark Zeidman,
Nephew

EXTENDED CIRCLE

Lance Bass,
Narrator

John Chambers,
Filmmaker

Kandi D'Taille,
Drag Performer

Yeona Dacosta-Auld,
Nurse

Mical DeBrow,
GLAD President

Frankie,
Drag Performer

Raydra Hall,
Filmmaker

David W. Hylan,
Author and Activist

Mark S. King,
Author and Activist

Marquita,
Drag Performer

DeDe DeSantis
McClamroch,
sister of Joe DeSantis

Clint McCommon,
Filmmaker

Jamie Morris,
Philadelphia Staff

Marcus Spurlock,
HIV/AIDS Physician

ACT UP benefit at Enoch's Bar, Shreveport (1989). Pictured: Buddy Williamson, Domingo Leija, Robert Darrow, Dorothy Prime, Chuck Selber, Barton Gross, Joe DeSantis, Bianca Welsh, Deborah Harold Allen, Joey Celmer, Kenny King, Tracy Murrell, Gary Cathey, Bonnie Parks, Erin Harold, and Alana Oldham.

AIDS activists group forms here

Holds four-hour session with LSUMC dean to discuss research differences

By LAURA BEIL
Journal Medical Writer

The AIDS activist group whose members are known for barricading themselves in the offices of a drug company and holding a "die-in" on the grounds of the state office building in New Orleans has come to Northwest Louisiana.

AIDS Coalition to Unleash Power has been quietly gathering steam over the past month, collecting information and plotting strategy at weekly meetings. Monday evening, after having faxed gripe letters to LSU Medical Center and the state Office of Public Health, ACT-UP members met for nearly four hours with Dr. Darryl Williams, the dean of the medical school, and Dr. John King, acting section chief of infectious diseases.

The group's main interest is in developing research and getting treatment for people with AIDS. It is given credit for bullying Burroughs Wellcome into cutting by 20 percent the price of AZT, a drug that prolongs the life of most AIDS patients but still costs several hundred dollars a month. Many of the changes in the way experimental drugs are distributed were a result of the government bending to the demands of ACT-UP. Indeed, their first local action at LSU Medical Center was a formal complaint about the medical school's foot-dragging in providing experimental drugs to local patients.

In a Dec. 8 letter faxed to Williams, ACT-UP members said they were "outraged that LSU Medical School in Shreveport did not elect to participate in the Tulane-LSU clinical trial unit . . ." Tulane University recently made international headlines with the announcement they had vaccinated nine monkeys

Act-Up's logo

with a simian AIDS vaccine. Responding to the letter, Williams called for a meeting with ACT-UP members to hammer out their differences.

That meeting began at 4 p.m. Monday. Three ACT-UP members showed up armed with bulging file folders of information, and before it was over Williams would cancel other obligations and call in his department chair for infectious dis-

Please See GROUP, Page 19A

Journal photo by Ed Barham

ACT-UP members Debbie Harold (left), Gary Cathey and Joe DeSantis sit in on the board meeting of the Greater Louisiana AIDS Defense.

The Shreveport Journal, December 20, 1989. Coverage of a four-hour meeting with the LSU Medical Center dean and announcement of ACT UP's formation.
Pictured: Deborah Harold Allen, Gary Cathey, and Joe DeSantis, shown here being removed from a GLAD meeting in a separate action.

ACT UP strategy meeting (1990). Back row, left to right: Dale Lancaster, Richard Kightlinger, Chuck Selber, Royce Stoope, Kurt Pickett, Kenny King, Deborah Harold Allen, Domingo Leija, and Cecil Thad Coburn. Front row: Joe DeSantis, James Smith, and Unknown.

ACT UP mayoral forum (1990), B'nai Zion Temple (Shreveport, LA).
Organized by ACT UP, mayoral candidates face questions from ACT UP members and a packed audience, the room charged with urgency and accountability.

Christmas party and benefit at the Florentine Club (1990).
Left to right: Chuck Selber, Deborah Harold Allen, and Billy Smith.

ACT UP New Year's Eve party at Chuck Selber's home (1990). Left to right: Deborah Harold Allen, Buddy Williamson, Chris Free, Chuck Selber, and Vern Ransburg.

DR. DAVID W. HYLAN

Ultimate Appearances Open House party (1991).
Chuck arrived with a notebook in hand, turning even a party into a platform.
Left to right: Tracy Murrell, Chuck Selber, and Deborah Harold Allen.

Pickle Barrel sit-in protest of the firing of Vern Ransburg (1990). Pictured: Joe DeSantis, Deborah Harold Allen, Judy Blue, Richard Kightlinger, Bruce Young, Buddy Williamson, and Chuck Selber. Not pictured: Alana Oldham, Robert Darrow, and Anthony O'Neil Hill.

ACT UP information booth. Chuck Selber.

Storm the NIH (1990). ACT UP members carry the banner leading the protest.
Left to right: Gary Cathey, Alana Oldham, Chuck Selber, and Robert Darrow.

　　　　　　　　　DR. DAVID W. HYLAN

Storm the NIH (1990).
Robert Darrow (center) raises his fist in protest among fellow demonstrators.

Storm the NIH (1990).
Alana Oldham and Joe DeSantis protest alongside fellow demonstrators.

CDC protest, Atlanta, Georgia (1990).
Robert Darrow (left of center) carries a sign reading "Jewel White died ..." surrounded
by the ACT UP Shreveport delegation. Credit: Dwight Ross, Jr.

Black banner displayed at the CDC protest (1990).

          DR. DAVID W. HYLAN

CDC protest, Atlanta, Georgia (1990).

Press conference demanding the resignation of the LSU Chancellor (1990).
Left to right: Robert Darrow, Alana Oldham, Chuck Selber, Jewel White, and Kenny King.
Not pictured: Deborah Harold Allen and Joe DeSantis.

Outing of Jim McCrery (1992).
Gary Cathey (far right) speaks with reporters
as ACT UP activists forced the issue into public view.

Journal photo by Scott Edwards

Boycott — Members of Act Up, The Sheveport Aids Coalition to Unleash Power, staged a beer boycott here Friday to protest contributions by Miller Brewing as one of the corporate donors to Sen. Jesse Helms' re-election campaign and a museum being built in N. Carolina to honor him.

The Shreveport Journal, September 29, 1990. Miller Beer protest at Thrifty Liquor.
Pictured: Camile LeGrand, Unknown, Alana Oldham, and Charlsa Henderson.

     DR. DAVID W. HYLAN

Protest on the menu — Members of Dukebusters protest Tuesday in front of a local restaurant whose owner contributed to the campaign of U.S. Senate candidate David Duke, a former Ku Klux Klan leader. The protestors, (left to right) Larry Crynes, John Csonks, Robert McLane, Charles Selber and Russel Wingfield, vow to continue picketing daily.

The Shreveport Journal, April 25, 1990. "Dukebusters" protest of David Duke.
Left to right: Larry Crynes, John Csonks, Robert McLane, Chuck Selber, and Russel Wingfield.

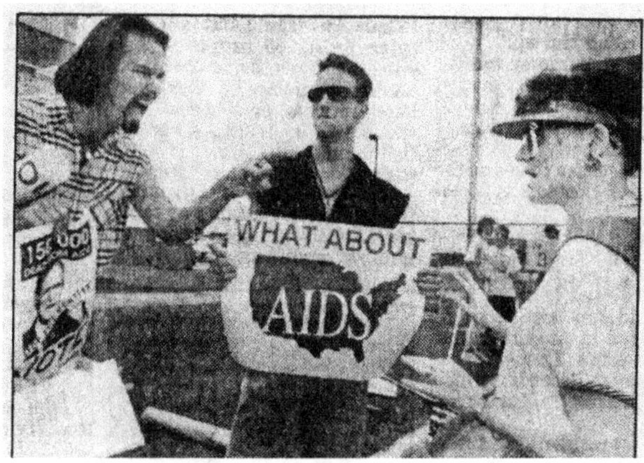

Kurt Pickett of Shreveport ACT UP argues about the president's lack of support on the AIDS issue with a Bush supporter who wished not to be identified. Chad Cromer holds the sign.

The Times, September 23, 1992. Kurt Pickett, Chad Cromer, and a Bush supporter.
© The Shreveport Times – USA TODAY NETWORK via Imagn Images

March on Washington for Lesbian, Gay, and Bi Equal Rights and Liberation (1993).
While visiting congressional offices during the march, Gary Cathey hands
a staff member for Congressman Jim McCrery his personal letter.

March on Washington for Lesbian, Gay, and Bi Equal Rights and Liberation (1993).
Justin Normand and Gary Cathey hold an enlarged three-dollar bill
depicting Congressman Jim McCrery, invoking the adage "fake as a three-dollar bill."

DR. DAVID W. HYLAN

KKK rally at the Caddo Courthouse (1993).
Kurt Pickett kisses another ACT UP protester in front of local Klansmen.

Names Project AIDS Memorial Quilt display at the Bossier Civic Center (1991).

The Shreveport Times, July 6, 1991. AIDS Quilt display at the Bossier City Convention Center. Justin Normand embraces his husband, Gary Cathey, in a moment of grief.
© The Shreveport Times – USA TODAY NETWORK via Imagn Images

AIDS Quilt display at the Bossier City Civic Center (1991). Chuck Selber pushes Richard Kightlinger in a wheelchair as they view more than 850 quilt panels.

DR. DAVID W. HYLAN

Chuck Selber's quilt panel. Chuck Selber's nieces and nephews hold the panel.
Left to right: Leslie Zeidman Snelgrove, Nancy Zeidman Accardo (front), Jill Selber Handaly,
Sandy Selber Sturm, Mark Zeidman, and Jay Zeidman.

Unplanned reunion at George's Grill (1992). Pictured: Richard Kightlinger, Greg Tolman,
Kurt Pickett, Robert Darrow, and Richard Williams.

George's Grill, Shreveport, Louisiana (2020).

The Philadelphia Center, Shreveport, Louisiana (2026).

    DR. DAVID W. HYLAN

Filming an interview for Small Town Rage (2013).
Bill and Jean Darrow, parents of Robert Darrow.

Recording session, The Nook Studio (Los Angeles, CA) (2016).
Left to right: Raydra Hall, Lance Bass, and David Hylan during the recording of
Lance Bass's narration for *Small Town Rage: Fighting Back in the Deep South.*

Irving and Flo Selber, Chuck Selber's parents, whose lives were forever shaped by their son's journey and the crisis that followed. Their backyard, late 1970s.

CHAPTER 6
SILENCE AND EXPOSURE

"If you choose to represent us, then represent all of us."
—ACT UP Shreveport Press Release, 1993

In the early 1990s, the silence they faced in Washington and Atlanta was nothing compared to the one at home. In Shreveport, that silence had a name, a title, and a seat in Congress. Representative Jim McCrery embodied everything they had been shouting against: hypocrisy wrapped in politeness, morality used as a shield. First elected to Congress in 1988, McCrery built a career on quiet influence, his power growing even as the people he represented were dying in silence. What began as whispers among friends became a question shouted through bullhorns: how long could a man vote against their lives while living a lie of his own?

Across the country, that same hypocrisy had become its own form of violence. Activists had whispered for years about congressmen and governors who slipped into restrooms and backrooms, then stood on the floors of Congress and in statehouses to deny AIDS funding, block civil rights, and legislate queer people into silence.

In the late 1980s and early 1990s, the ethics of outing were argued as fiercely as any policy debate. In the documentary *Outrage* (2009), activist Michael Rogers framed the rationale without apology: "I'm not outing people who are gay. I'm reporting on individuals who are working against the community who then expect that community to protect them." Congressman Barney Frank, interviewed in the same film, distilled the counterweight into a single sentence: "There is a right to privacy but not a right to hypocrisy."

To many, coming out remained sacred, an act of timing and self-ownership. But when a man cloaks himself in silence while voting against AIDS research funding, denying LGBTQ+ rights, or propping up the very bigotry that keeps him hidden, that silence becomes something more than privacy. It becomes complicity. That silence was not abstract. It had shape. It could be seen, felt, and measured in the spaces where something should have been—but wasn't.

For Gary Cathey, coming out had always been understood as something personal—something that belonged to the individual, not to be taken or forced. But McCrery's public life began to reshape that principle. The issue was no longer private. It had consequences. Gary's knowledge of McCrery was not secondhand—it came from personal experience, from an encounter that stood in direct contradiction to the positions McCrery would later take in public office. And long before 1992—long before ACT UP—he believed that truth needed to be told. When McCrery first emerged as a right-wing Republican candidate in 1987, Gary tried to act. He reached out to local media, contacting KSLA news director Jack Hodges, only to be met with dismissal and open hostility. He attempted to pass information through political channels during McCrery's first campaign, even approaching people connected to his opponent, Foster Campbell. But there was no path forward. No one would act. The truth existed—but it had nowhere to land.

"My first sexual experience was with McCrery," Gary would later say, tracing it back to a summer night at the Sigma Nu fraternity house at Louisiana Tech University in Ruston, Louisiana. The campus had thinned out for the season. Most students were gone, including Gary's roommate. The house, usually loud with movement and voices, had settled into a quieter rhythm.

Gary had already gone to bed. The lights were off. The room held the stillness of late- night, the kind that comes when there is nothing left to interrupt it.

At some point, McCrery came in and pulled a chair up beside the bed, positioning it level with Gary's waist, and began talking. The

     DR. DAVID W. HYLAN

conversation itself did not feel unusual at first—two fraternity brothers in a familiar space, the cadence of voices low in the dark. Then, without warning, the tone shifted. McCrery leaned forward and rested his head against Gary's crotch.

What followed was immediate and unannounced.

Gary was caught off guard—shocked by both the suddenness and the certainty of it. There had been no conversation leading to this, no signal that the moment was coming. He did not stop him. He allowed it to continue, even as the surprise of it stayed with him.

Nothing about it was spoken aloud—not before, not during, not after. But the terms were understood. What had happened would not be discussed. It would not be repeated to anyone.

That silence became part of the experience itself.

What began that night became a pattern—more than a decade of secrecy that blurred friendship and desire.

In New York, Gary had seen a different world taking shape. At the Pyramid Club in the East Village, the room held something not yet fully visible but already undeniable. Performers like Blondie and Madonna passed through that space before they became international names, part of a culture that was still forming in real time. It wasn't polished. It wasn't widely accepted. But it was happening. Music blurred genres, gender blurred presentation, and the future felt present—unfolding in front of him. Standing there, Gary believed something was changing, even if the rest of the country had not caught up. McCrery did not. He dismissed it entirely, brushing it off as nothing new, nothing meaningful. Where Gary saw a world emerging, McCrery saw nothing worth acknowledging.

At times McCrery tried to recast their sexual relationship as a kind of higher brotherhood, but for Gary it was never just a fraternity game. It was a bond that carried weight—and a wound that deepened when McCrery remade himself as a Republican Christian coalition candidate, renouncing those who lived publicly what he had framed as a higher brotherhood in private.

Gary's story was not the only one. A second former fraternity brother, who spoke on the condition of anonymity, offered his own testimony. He said McCrery had pursued him in college and that years later they had sex in Dallas after McCrery sought out a gay bar. He also described how Sigma Nu helped keep McCrery's behavior quiet. When another student tried to report McCrery's advances—to both the police and the university administration—fraternity leaders pressured him to stay silent until he finally quit school. "They all tried to hush it up," the witness recalled, naming the men who closed ranks around McCrery. McCrery denied his own life while Gary took the wrath—enduring smear campaigns and exile as McCrery's political career moved forward untouched.

The Advocate, the national gay and lesbian newsmagazine, published its September 1992 cover story, "The Outing of a Family Values Congressman." According to that reporting, a Dallas high school teacher who asked not to be named said he had known McCrery since their Louisiana Tech years and later slept with him twice in 1987—just months before McCrery first ran for Congress in 1988.

In one account, McCrery called while in Dallas on political business, came to his apartment, and spent the night. The same man recalled riding in a car with McCrery and Dallas contractor Larry Locke when McCrery urged them to head to the gay bars.

Larry remembered the moment clearly: "He didn't seem to have any trouble being gay. It was just assumed that the three of us were." *The magazine* also quoted another Louisiana Tech alumnus, also speaking anonymously and now living outside Louisiana, who said he too had slept with McCrery—once in the congressman's apartment and once in the backseat of a car—and quoted McCrery as saying he could "have the best of both worlds because I can love anyone."

At the same time, McCrery's personal life was taking shape in public in a quieter way. There was no national announcement, no spectacle— just the familiar rhythm of local reporting. A marriage. A photograph. A short column noting the union, placed alongside other community updates that marked stability, respectability, and order.

In a city like Shreveport, that kind of announcement carried its own language. It did not argue. It did not explain. It simply reassured.

For many watching, the image did its work. A wife. A public life that aligned cleanly with the values being spoken from podiums and pulpits. Whatever questions had surfaced in the months before did not disappear—but they were pushed to the edges, made easier to ignore.

The narrative did not have to be proven—only accepted.

That truth did not vanish because a ring was placed on a finger. It remained in the roll-call votes, the floor speeches, the budget lines, and the rider amendments. A hospital bed withheld; a lab test unfunded; a funeral hastened by policy. McCrery had made those choices. *The*

     DR. DAVID W. HYLAN

Advocate had printed them. Gary had lived them. And for those who stood inside that moment, the clarity of it would not remain untouched.

Years later, not everyone who stood there would remember it without complication.

Judy Williams, who had been part of the protests and had spoken to a reporter during the controversy, would come to see one piece of it differently. At the time, she had acted out of urgency and conviction—like many others—driven by what she saw as indifference to a crisis already claiming lives.

But time shifted how she understood her role in the outing itself. "That was unkind of me," she said later. "It wasn't for me to out him. That decision—to come out—belongs to the individual."

She did not step away from the fight. She continued to organize, to speak out, and to challenge the decisions she believed were costing lives—including helping lead a public response with a group of other women against McCrery's voting record, his opposition to AIDS funding and prevention, and his refusal to support LGBTQ+ rights.

What changed was not her understanding of the urgency, but of the boundary. The confrontation remained, even as the question of how far to go did not settle as easily.

Early in the organizing of ACT UP Shreveport, as actions began to take form, Chuck Selber began pressing Gary to out McCrery. The pressure did not arrive all at once. It built with every vote McCrery cast—against AIDS funding, against prevention programs, against anything that acknowledged the lives of the people ACT UP was fighting for. Each vote tightened the question until it could no longer be ignored. Gary had already made up his mind about the truth. What held him back was not whether to tell it, but what it would cost once he did. Chuck pushed relentlessly. Gary did not resist the idea—he resisted the consequences.

The conflict did not play out in public meetings. It unfolded privately, in repeated conversations—often between Gary and Chuck alone. They spoke about it again and again, sometimes calmly, sometimes not. Chuck's urgency came from the bodies he was watching disappear. Gary's hesitation came from knowing exactly what exposure would cost. In one conversation that stayed with him, Chuck described making a deal—securing a promise about votes in exchange for neutralizing Gary. The tone was not collaborative. It was sharp, condescending, and deeply personal. Chuck was dying. Gary was not. And in that imbalance, compassion gave way to pressure.

Within that pressure, ACT UP argued—not like a parliament with gavels and rules, but like a family that had too much to lose. At times, Gary was moved to tears, torn between a past he could not deny and the funerals he could no longer bear to attend. To out the congressman would be to out himself—to upend his own family and invite everything that followed: suspicion, cruelty, exile. "I never even had a conversation with my parents about my sexuality until I knew the outing was going to make national news," he later recalled. "I was thirty-six years old when I finally sat with my parents and grandparents and told them why I was having to do what I was doing publicly."

Gary spoke of the force that met his hesitation. If he felt the weight of history, Chuck felt the urgency of it. Chuck had no tolerance left for caution. In those meetings, he made it plain: waiting meant more people would die. Robert Darrow described how Chuck's voice cut through the room—sharp, uncompromising. Deborah added that restraint was a luxury people with AIDS did not have. In his play *Defense of the Committee*, Chuck stripped away excuses with a single line: "We are dying while you debate."

As Gary later put it: "Silence wasn't neutral. It took sides."

By then, he had come to understand that quiet did not simply protect McCrery—it protected the lie. McCrery's private denials had become inseparable from his public power, and every vote against AIDS funding, every speech dressed in moral certainty, pressed that silence into service. Gary did not see himself as exposing a man's private life. He saw himself confronting a pattern of dishonesty with consequences measured not in headlines, but in hospital beds and obituaries.

Alana remembered how sharp that debate had become—and how much of it turned on Gary's vulnerability. "Chuck wanted Gary to out McCrery, and that's a really big ask," she said. "Gary probably needed time to think about that, because that's massive. You're talking about outing a United States Congressman." Once Gary spoke, there would be no way back to anonymity, safety, or ordinary life.

He understood those consequences intimately. He had grown up in small Louisiana towns where difference was not debated but punished, where rumors traveled faster than truth, and violence often arrived wearing righteousness. To speak publicly would not only expose McCrery; it would expose Gary's parents, his family name, and the land they lived on to scrutiny and threat. Silence had once felt like protection—not just for himself, but for everyone tethered to him.

That memory carried the weight of loss. He understood why Chuck felt the way he did, and that understanding did not lessen the damage between them. "I understood why Chuck hated me for not being brave enough to do what I knew I was supposed to do," Gary said. "Because I hated myself." The distance that opened between them never closed. Chuck died with that rupture unresolved, and Gary was left carrying the grief.

The loss of Chuck sharpened what Gary already knew: waiting did not pause the crisis. People kept dying while arguments stayed theoretical. What had once felt like an unbearable decision began to feel like an unavoidable one.

As ACT UP member Richard Kightlinger later recalled, the two men were like oil and water—but even so, they still found ways to support each other when it mattered. Alana's memory was gentler. "This issue probably caused a bit of conflict there between Gary and Chuck. I really believe that Chuck, in his heart, didn't hate Gary—didn't hold a grudge."

Gary once put it another way: "Through my time with that, I was close to Chuck. I had threatened to run against McCrery and use the act of being a candidate against him as the vehicle to out him and to discuss what his votes were doing to our community."

Taken together, the pressure was not theoretical. It was enforced, negotiated, and often disguised as protection. It looked like absence. It sounded like nothing. And it carried weight.

What made the decision unavoidable was the widening gulf between his private life and his public record. In Washington, his votes carried consequences that were already visible at home. In Shreveport, those same votes translated into empty beds, closed doors, and funerals that multiplied without pause. Gary carried the private truth of McCrery's intimacy; ACT UP carried the public consequences of his actions. To speak that truth would put Gary's own life under a microscope, and everyone in the room understood it. Deborah Allen said the contradiction was impossible to ignore: "McCrery's policies didn't reflect his sexual orientation at all. He was voting against AIDS funding to mask that he was gay himself."

Even before the cover story hit, the consequences of speaking openly were already clear. When Buddy Williamson's small community magazine, *Tri-State Tea*, ran stories exposing McCrery, the response was violent in its own way. Copies were not just discarded—they were gathered.

Late one evening, outside Central Station, a group of women stepped out into the dark carrying stacks of *Tri-State Tea*. The air was thick and still, the kind of Southern night that holds heat long after the sun has disappeared. Someone struck a lighter. The first copies curled inward almost immediately, ink blackening, paper tightening as the flames took hold.

Others came out of the bar with more issues in their hands—copies pulled from tables, counters, wherever they had been left behind. One by one, they fed them into the fire. No one rushed. No one joked. It was deliberate.

Inside, the music continued. Outside, the glow of burning pages lit the edges of faces watching in silence.

Word traveled quickly. By the next day, Buddy Williamson knew something had happened—not from a formal report, but from absence. Copies that should have been there were gone. In a community that small, disappearance was its own kind of message.

The flames confirmed what ACT UP already understood: exposing McCrery would not only provoke political backlash—it would fracture the fragile alliances within their own community.

That morning, members walked into McCrery's Shreveport district office carrying two things: a formal ACT UP Shreveport press release and a fresh copy of the magazine. Gary's written statement would come later, when he returned from Dallas and delivered it himself. Once those materials crossed the threshold, there would be no retreat—no private version of Gary left untouched by what followed.

They distributed copies of *The Advocate* to local media and laid out McCrery's voting record on AIDS funding and gay rights. The focus was policy, not biography—roll call votes, appropriations blocked, research denied, protections opposed. This was ACT UP's statement as a movement.

Kurt Pickett stepped forward to speak. He did not improvise. He read from a prepared statement—measured, direct, and unflinching: "SILENCE = DEATH... ACT UP is a diverse, non-partisan group of individuals united in anger and committed to direct action to end the AIDS crisis."

But he did not stop there. What followed moved quickly from definition to confrontation. Citing a national exposé from *The Advocate*, Kurt named Congressman Jim McCrery directly—describing what ACT

UP saw as a double life and condemning a voting record that opposed AIDS funding, prevention efforts, and access to information. He pointed to delays in federal assistance, the suppression of Surgeon General C. Everett Koop's educational materials, and the measurable human cost—shortened life expectancies, rising infection rates, and a growing number of women and children affected in McCrery's own district.

The argument was deliberate: not rumor, not speculation, but documented action. His record was not abstract. He opposed AIDS funding, resisted prevention efforts—including needle-exchange programs—and used his platform to undermine public health messaging. At one point, he used taxpayer-funded mailings to warn parents against federally distributed AIDS education materials, urging them to destroy the information before their children could read it.

The words carried across the parking lot, landing with more weight than volume. The air was still, every movement visible within a few feet. This was not spectacle. It was indictment.

"We support truth and honesty," the statement declared. "History will judge McCrery... not for being gay... but for participating in the oppression and destruction of his own people."

Members stood beside him holding copies of *The Advocate*. They stood in the open air outside McCrery's district office, the building behind them, the lot exposed to anyone passing by. Some watched the small group of reporters. Others watched the office door.

Gary was not there—not yet. His absence was felt—not as a gap in the message, but as a line not yet crossed. He was already pulling away from it, even before he arrived. When he would later stand in front of cameras outside the office, part of him would feel removed—as if watching the moment happen to someone else. The words would come, but through distance, through the realization that nothing about his life would remain private after that point.

A few days later, Gary drove in from Dallas to do something separate—and more personal. He did not even have the money to make the trip. To get there, he pawned a ring he had owned since high school—a tiger-eye set with diamonds, something he had once worn for special occasions. He never got it back. That was the cost of the drive that would change everything. The highway stretched longer than the miles suggested. It cut through long stretches of North Louisiana—pine and open road, the same landscape he had known most of his life—but it did not feel familiar. This was no longer a discussion, no longer a question to be debated in meetings. The road gave him too much time to think. Mile after mile, there was no one to interrupt the argument in his head—no Chuck, no meetings, no voices but his own. The same questions circled back again and again, each time with less room to avoid them. By the time he crossed into Shreveport, the decision had already been made.

Before he stood in front of any camera, there was nothing left to resolve. The conversations that needed to happen had already happened. The truth had already been spoken in the rooms that mattered most.

Now, what remained was public.

McCrery went on television in Louisiana and told reporters, "I am not homosexual," dismissing the allegations as lies pushed by extremists. He insisted the controversy was a smear campaign—a desperate attempt to undercut his re-election—and promised supporters he would not step aside, vowing to stay in the race and keep his focus on what he called "pertinent issues."

McCrery's public record told its own story. Scorecards at the time showed sharp contrasts: Americans for Democratic Action rated him at twelve percent, while the American Conservative Union gave him a ninety-four. The National Gay and Lesbian Task Force marked his fall from sixty-four percent in 1990 to fourteen percent in 1991. The Human Rights Campaign Fund tracked an even sharper decline—from eighty percent in 1989 to zero in 1991. Behind those numbers were concrete votes: to keep the immigration ban on gays and lesbians; to oppose nondiscrimination protections in employment and education; to block federal funds for research that could have informed HIV prevention; to cut AIDS research; to preserve military sodomy laws. In letters to constituents, he warned that the Surgeon General's nationwide AIDS brochure was "permissive" and "abnormal." An editorial in *The Shreveport Journal* called that rhetoric "utter demagoguery." Those votes were not abstractions. They were the difference between a bed and a hallway, between medicine and waiting, between a funeral next month and a funeral next week.

He also aligned himself with efforts to block harm-reduction strategies, including federal support for needle-exchange programs—measures that public health experts had already shown could reduce HIV transmission. To activists, those positions were not abstract moral stances. They were decisions with measurable consequences.

Alana Oldham framed it in terms of betrayal. To her, McCrery was not just another conservative vote in Washington; he was a man who knew better—who lived among people carrying the weight of AIDS and yet chose to legislate as if their lives were expendable. "He wasn't uninformed," she said. "He knew the truth and voted against it anyway."

The silence inside Sigma Nu fraternity was not the only shield around McCrery. As covered by *The Shreveport Times* during the 1992 re-election race, he was measured not by the whispers but by the horse race.

One column rated Jerry Huckaby, his Democratic challenger, and McCrery side by side, as if the only question were who could pull ahead. Poll numbers and strategy filled the page, while the whispers remained background noise—part of the tally, not the story.

If the newspapers spoke in code, *Tri-State Tea* did not. In the months leading up to the September 1992 cover story in *The Advocate*, the column passed between friends and colleagues, its tone less about proof than performance. What the daily papers couched in polls and strategy, Buddy's *Tri-State Tea* splashed with a wink and a smirk. Every sly aside made McCrery's denials sound thinner, every rumor a little harder to shake.

Meanwhile, not all the jabs came in whispers. As *The Shreveport Times* reported, a third candidate, Robbert Thompson, was said to be "nipping at the big two." Thompson never had the money or the machinery to win, but his presence mattered. It suggested McCrery's advantage was more fragile than it appeared—one revelation away from collapse.

Cornered, McCrery lashed out. He blasted his opponents and *The Shreveport Times*, railing against what he called a vicious smear. Each denial came sharpened with accusation, casting criticism as persecution and framing himself as the target of unfair attacks.

It was a familiar strategy: turn defense into performance, outrage into armor. On the stump, McCrery cast himself as the victim of lies, betrayed by rivals and unfairly targeted. The louder he spoke, the more he leaned into that role—a candidate sustained not by proof, but by the force of his denial.

And yet, for all the visible fractures, McCrery rose. The race gathered momentum, grinding past scandal and whispers alike. Poll numbers steadied, then crept upward, convincing enough voters that he was the wronged man in a dirty fight.

By then, McCrery had firmly planted himself in the Republican ascendancy. He aligned with conservative groups such as Oliver North's campaign and the Eagle Forum and was applauded as the 1992 Republican National Convention framed the election as a culture war. From the convention floor, as Pat Buchanan thundered against homosexual rights, delegates waved signs reading "FAMILY VALUES FOREVER / GAY RIGHTS NEVER." Gary watched, stunned, knowing the private truth of the man in the suit. "The McCrery I see now doesn't stand up for what he is," he told *The Advocate*.

He wrapped himself in the language of family values, of tradition and faith. His allies closed ranks, protecting the image. Every endorsement, every handshake, every carefully managed appearance reinforced that stability.

To the public eye, McCrery looked untouchable—a candidate who had endured the worst and emerged intact. To those who knew the silences behind the headlines, it was a triumph built on denial.

The campaign pressed on as if exposure were merely a distraction. As coverage began to fade, *The Shreveport Times* quoted McCrery telling supporters it was time to "turn focus to pertinent issues." He doubled down on his platform of family values and fiscal conservatism, acting as though nothing had shifted. ACT UP Shreveport refused to let him reset the conversation. They issued statements and staged actions that tied every speech and every vote back to the epidemic. One release called the AIDS issue "a strong case against McCrery," pointing not to rumor but to roll call votes and appropriations that had starved research and left people without care.

What finally shifted was not courage, but endurance. Gary could no longer carry the contradiction without being reshaped by it. McCrery's public certainty depended on Gary's private restraint. Each day Gary stayed silent, the lie grew sturdier; each day he waited, the damage spread outward. The question was no longer whether telling the truth would cost him everything—it was whether not telling it had already done so.

Standing there, Gary felt the finality settle in. This was not vindication; it was surrender—to truth, to consequence, to whatever followed. He understood that McCrery would survive this moment far more easily than he would.

The silence that followed was heavier than any protest chant. Robert later spoke about the sting of humiliation—how quickly the word "terrorist" was hurled at anyone who dared to speak. Gary felt it land almost at once.

Gary had expected that result. He understood that the town would protect itself before it protected him, that the discomfort of truth would be redirected toward the person who spoke it. Friends grew cautious. Doors closed softly rather than slamming. Invitations thinned, then stopped. What followed was not a single punishment, but a gradual narrowing—a life made smaller.

In one moment that stayed with him, Gary heard what that narrowing sounded like out loud. In a local store, within earshot but not spoken to him directly, a man asked, "Whatever happened to the Cathey boy? Is he dead yet?" Another man, standing nearby, answered without hesitation: "Well, ask him—he's standing right here." The words shifted the space instantly. What had been spoken as rumor became immediate, unavoidable. Gary was no longer something distant to be speculated about. He was present. Seen. And, in that moment, exposed in a way that left no room for retreat.

Nancy Morris Cook, a journalist in Shreveport, drew the line even more starkly. "There was not a single thing McCrery ever said that I could agree with," she said later. "Did he deserve to be silenced? Yes."

The fallout arrived with the inevitability of weather. Gary's motives were questioned, and his name was dragged through rooms where he had once felt safe. In August 1991, before the outing would become national news, McCrery staged a familiar defense: a courtship, a marriage to Johnette—a young television anchor—a tableau of heterosexual reassurance.

The town adjusted without admitting it had changed. Churches began to speak more carefully, if not more openly. Hospitals became less avoidant, if not more compassionate. Conversations that once stopped at implication edged closer to acknowledgment. The silence did not disappear, but it loosened—just enough to let something else through.

Gary's voice, when he spoke about those memories later, carried no triumph. "I lost my community. Everything," he said. The cost was not theoretical. It was immediate and enduring. The people he had grown up with, the spaces that had once felt like home, the quiet familiarity of belonging—all of it shifted. What had once been ordinary became contested, then inaccessible.

The funerals did not stop, but the silence that had protected men like McCrery no longer held. What had once been contained began to move—through conversations, through confrontations, through people who refused to disappear. The names multiplied. The voices grew louder. And from that fracture, something else took shape—visible, uncontained, and impossible to ignore: a cast of rage.

CHAPTER 7
CAST OF RAGE

"Put us in a room and you'd swear we didn't belong together. Put us in the streets and you couldn't look away."
—Buddy Williamson, ACT UP Shreveport member

The story of that moment—the outing—does not belong to one person. It did not end when the words were spoken or when the headlines faded. What it revealed, instead, was who would carry the weight that followed—who would stay, who would speak, and who would refuse silence. These were not people who arrived as leaders. They became them because no one else stepped forward. Many of those decisions were made in borrowed rooms—apartments with ashtrays full, kitchen tables crowded with flyers and coffee cups, voices stretching late into the night as plans took shape.

This is the cast of rage.

What followed was not clarity but consequence. Shreveport did not erupt or repent. It absorbed. Voices lowered. Questions went unasked. Exposure stripped away illusion but left power intact, revealing how carefully power protects itself. ACT UP Shreveport understood that spectacle was never the finish line. The fight would not hinge on one man's duplicity but on whether they could keep pressing truth into systems built to deflect it. This was the work after rage—steadier, less visible, and more dangerous. It required persistence and pressure that could not be ignored.

They were not celebrities or polished spokespeople. They were men and women from North Louisiana whose lives collided with a crisis that demanded more of them. Rage struck the match. What came next was commitment—showing up when it would have been easier to stay home, speaking when silence was safer, refusing to let the city's comfort do the killing. Each stepped into the gap and held it open. The lives gathered here are not arranged by importance. There was no hierarchy of sacrifice. Each person worked, risked, and stood up when the larger world chose silence. Their stories unfold in narrative order, not in the order of their worth.

Energy often coalesced around a sharp-edged presence: Gary Cathey, restless at the edge of a room and quick to cut through hypocrisy. He arrived early and saw clearly, not because he was prophetic, but because he paid attention.

Born in 1956, in Shreveport and raised across small Louisiana towns, eventually landing in Minden, he learned young how to read a room and survive being labeled before he understood the charge. The word sissy followed him; so did expectation.

He grew into leadership, serving as Louisiana Tech's Student Government Association president before leaving for New York, where fashion sharpened his instincts and survival refined them. When AIDS began hollowing out that world, he volunteered with Gay Men's Health Crisis, washing men abandoned by nurses, working in rooms where the air hung still and close. He moved slowly, careful with bodies that had grown light beneath his hands, the silence broken only by water and breath. Sometimes, a patient would lean back into his touch, and for a moment the work became something else: not treatment, but care.

By late 1989, back in Louisiana, he helped spark ACT UP Shreveport with Chuck and Joe, reading Jim McCrery's rhetoric for what it was. "If we're polite about this," he'd say, "we'll be polite all the way to the cemetery."

Outing McCrery cost him community, but not conviction. Years later, Gary would say he did not see the outing as a success. McCrery

     DR. DAVID W. HYLAN

was reelected again and again, and the votes never changed. For him, the outcome did not match the risk.

When he marched behind the ACT UP banner at the 1990 NIH protest in Bethesda, it was never about headlines. It was about keeping the dying in view.

That insistence did not end with the protests. Decades later, when Gary spoke to students at the Louisiana School for Math, Science, and the Arts, the past returned in a different form. The following year, those students came back with a panel for the AIDS Memorial Quilt, dedicated to a man he had spoken about. He called it one of the proudest moments of his life. What had once been loss returned as recognition—not complete, not repaired, but acknowledged.

Not everyone who carried that banner carried it the same way. Some arrived through fury; others through devotion.

Raised in Natchitoches amid oil-field wealth and rigid Baptist isolation, Justin Normand knew early the contradictions of North Louisiana—privilege and violence, faith and fear. After his father's sudden death and years of abuse, he left home at sixteen, carrying belief and defiance.

By the time he met Gary in 1991, he had already wrestled with silence in his own life, coming out in Memphis after a nervous call to a gay switchboard and discovering in Dallas that shame had lied to him about his worth. ACT UP felt less like rebellion than alignment.

He cut and pasted flyers, helped move AIDS Memorial Quilt panels, and worked alongside Gary as the group pushed private hypocrisy into public view, including a late stop at a Dallas Kinko's before heading back to Shreveport after eleven that night, where strategy met glue, paper, and urgency. He was not the loudest voice in the room, but he was steady. He understood cultivated ignorance because he had grown up inside it, and he believed privilege demanded use.

Justin and Gary remain together more than three decades later, their partnership continuing as both anchor and legacy. They divide their time between Dallas and Natchitoches, sharing a life shaped by historic preservation, their dogs, and a shared appreciation for the lives they have built together.

Illness became theater in a garage apartment in Houston, where playwright Chuck Selber turned dying into games for his nieces and nephews—building entire worlds out of blankets and chairs, turning rooms into forts where imagination outran what waited outside. He wrote the lines Shreveport did not want to say and made the city hear them anyway—*Defense of the Committee*, a play that forced Shreveport to confront what politeness tried to bury.

Trained at the Pasadena Playhouse and seasoned in New Orleans' experimental stages, Chuck believed theater was not escape but confrontation. He staged fashion shows before the city was ready, blurred the lines between performance and protest, and refused to let the word AIDS remain unsaid in polite company.

Jewish, gay, Southern, and unapologetic, Chuck was awkward and combustible, tender and difficult, often in the same hour. He could make you furious and make you laugh in the same breath, pushing past compromise when patience felt like surrender. Beneath the performance was devotion—to family, to truth, to the belief that art could crack open what politics sealed shut.

His mother, Flo, founded MAP, Mothers of AIDS Patients, turning grief into service, while Chuck kept creating, cleaning out boxes of mementos with a grin: "I just hope they don't find a cure after I throw all this stuff out."

He died in 1991 in Shreveport of AIDS-related illness, but what he made and dared outlived him.

Protest also had a body, and Joe DeSantis carried it. His hands, steady as he knotted twine through cardboard signs, bore the marks of someone the system had tried to discard: jail cells, bruises, and the cruelty of being told that gay men were disposable.

When he was jailed for public intoxication and disorderly conduct in Shreveport, guards discovered he was HIV-positive and chose humiliation over humanity, urinating on him in his cell. He survived it, but it marked him. When it was over, he stayed where he was, not trusting his body enough to move. The smell clung to him, deepening as the room stayed quiet. He said nothing, just held himself still, absorbing what had been done as if moving might make it real in a different way.

What was meant to break him became fuel. A gifted artist trained in Florence, he turned outrage into color and satire, cutting his mother's mink stole into chains for his show *Slave to Fashion*. At Artist Transit, he made beauty do hard labor, refusing to let grief and glamour live in separate rooms.

He could lift a room with a line, then gut it with the next, his humor not softness but a blade. When ACT UP called a press conference demanding the LSU chancellor's resignation, Joe sat directly behind Chuck, shoulder to shoulder with fellow members, forming a visible wall at his back.

By the end, his work darkened, but his refusal never did. Joe died in 1995 from AIDS-related complications, leaving behind paintings and memories that still hang in the homes of those he loved.

That balance of fire and steadiness made space for quieter voices, like Dr. Robert Darrow, who often sat at the back of meetings with a pen in hand, noting acronyms, circling trial names, and drawing arrows between treatments as if mapping a route through a minefield. Born and raised in Shreveport, shaped by teachers and preachers, he held leadership early but silence deeper, coming of age as a gay son in a Southern Baptist home where identity was negotiated carefully.

Diagnosed in 1985 at 27 years old, after a blood donation revealed what was then called HTLV-3, he received the news in a phone call from the blood bank—no counseling, no preparation, just a cold verdict left to settle. Three months, they told him. He prepared to die, making small gifts for friends and keeping a copy of *Final Exit* on his nightstand in case suffering overtook him.

Instead, he lived. Shock hardened into purpose, driven by the belief he might only have weeks left to live. He moved to New York, working nights in nightclub management and days volunteering with the Community Research Initiative on AIDS, where information became both lifeline and weapon.

A call from Chuck Selber pulled him back to Shreveport, where silence still ruled. There, he helped turn anger into infrastructure, co-founding the Philadelphia Center and serving as its first director, insisting that those closest to the crisis were not liabilities but leaders.

His voice, though soft, could cut through shouting without trying to outshout it. Survival became a form of leadership. Building became his method of resistance.

After decades directing the Shreveport Little Theatre, Robert retired with emeritus titles while continuing his advocacy on the board of the Philadelphia Center. He divides his time between Shreveport and New Orleans, living with his dog, Hermionne, who once belonged to his mother, Jean.

Kurt Pickett embodied precision and defiance. He was still a teenager when he found ACT UP Shreveport, joining the group in its earliest days at just seventeen. Clear, exact, and unflinching, he spoke with the authority of someone twice his age.

He had already survived the private war of coming out in the Deep South, pulled back from despair by a teacher who recognized the plea hidden in his journals and refused to let him disappear. From that moment, he chose visibility as discipline.

In photos, he is mid-shout at a George H. W. Bush supporter, his face lit with conviction. In meetings, he could level a room. Sitting across from the LSU Medical Center chancellor beside Bill Darrow, Robert Darrow's father and a steady presence through the worst years, he demanded answers for the mistreatment of AIDS patients, pressing until power blinked.

"Doctor, are you condescending to me?" he asked, and did not flinch when the man stammered. The moment captured what made him singular: youth carried with precision, fury delivered in complete sentences.

He joined bridge blockades and kiss-ins, fought hospital neglect, and turned every insult into oxygen.

Kurt died in 2009 from non-Hodgkin's lymphoma, remembered in the students and friends who still speak his name.

If Robert grounded the movement in fact, Deborah Allen grounded it in conscience. She carried a different kind of authority—conviction fused with the insistence that silence could not be allowed to stand. A teacher at heart, Deborah had been resisting conformity since childhood; at thirteen, she wrote to a jailed Vietnam War protester, her first act of dissent. Decades later, after losing a beloved friend, John David Horning, to AIDS and realizing her own fear had cost precious time, she made a vow: never again.

In late 1989, when Chuck, Joe, and Gary began meeting to form ACT UP Shreveport, she offered her apartment for the first gathering. From that moment, she became both anchor and amplifier, steady in purpose and fierce in protest.

She helped create the Philadelphia Center and worked with others to establish the region's first Viral Disease Clinic. Later, she carried that same mission into classrooms and civil rights work, preserving the stories of those who risked everything so others might live without shame.

She kept the group's fury tethered to its purpose. What she built did not stop when the marches ended; it carried forward in her work, her students, and in the family that learned early that activism is something you hand down.

That work carried forward long after the marches ended. Deborah remained in Shreveport, continuing her work centered on dignity, equity, and community care. She spent eight years with the ACLU of Louisiana and remains an active voice in HIV awareness, civil rights, and LGBTQ+ advocacy. Today, she works as a life coach, supporting underserved clients with guidance, empowerment, and practical tools for stability and growth. Her focus remains on those most often left out of systems of care—ensuring access, support, and a path forward. She continues to believe that true activism is a combination of love and anger, the two forces that drive lasting change.

Not every shift made noise.

Judy Williams moved through Shreveport in a world where reputation carried weight. A native of the city, educated at St. Vincent's Academy and Louisiana State University, she built her life inside the very structures that defined success in Northwest Louisiana—visibility, respectability, and the careful management of both. As founder of Williams Creative Group, a marketing and public relations firm she launched in 1989, she became one of the city's most recognized professional voices, later named a recipient of the 2000 ATHENA Leadership Award and one of the few admitted to the Public Relations Society of America College of Fellows.

She understood how messages were shaped, how perception held, how influence moved. When she acted, it was through that same language—writing letters, calling civic leaders and government officials, applying pressure not through spectacle but through persistence. ACT UP did not arrive in her life as performance. It arrived as interruption.

"It raised my consciousness," she said, "about the responsibility to speak up when something is wrong." The shift was not theatrical. It was internal, steady, and irreversible. In a city that rewarded conformity, she came to understand that silence was not neutrality but participation. The language of her profession—strategy, positioning, control—met something less containable: truth spoken without permission.

Her life carried both worlds at once. At twenty-six, she was writing dialogue for Orson Welles, hearing him stop a production to ask, "Who wrote this dialogue? It's great!" Years later, she would stand inside a different kind of script, one without rehearsal, where speaking carried consequence.

She sold her agency in 2018 but never stepped away from the work that followed. Her focus turned toward race relations, addiction, and the harder, less visible labor of community repair.

What ACT UP left with her was not a single act but a permanent shift: the understanding that dignity requires a voice—and that once found, it cannot be set aside.

Alana Oldham learned the cost of being seen. Born in Minden and raised to be polite, she discovered early that politeness could be a cage.

Modeling brought her to Fashion Euphoria, a fundraiser meant to help those living with AIDS—until the money was quietly redirected to a church. The betrayal sharpened her. When Chuck Selber returned from New York with ACT UP urgency, Alana, known then as Cristy, was among the first to join.

Barely eighteen, she stepped into a movement that did not shield its young. She worked tables and phone trees, printed and passed flyers, and stood at the Pickle Barrel protests after Vern Ransburg was fired, learning quickly what it meant to confront power in public.

She stood front and center in photos, disarming those who assumed activists came only in one form. After an ABC Channel 3 news segment outed her on television, she was at Joe DeSantis' house in Shreveport when her mother called, demanding that she contact the station and force a retraction. She went home instead. When she told her the truth—"I'm gay"—her mother slapped her and told her she could not stay. Within hours, friends helped gather her things and took her to a house on Youree Drive, where she found a temporary place to stay. Only later did she understand she had been couch surfing in a brothel. In the moment, it was simply somewhere to land.

"At the time, it didn't feel like we were making much difference," she later said. "But if we look back, we did. Things changed. Shreveport changed."

After two decades living in Europe, Alana now runs a small software company in New Orleans, building a life that reflects the independence she fought to claim. Her career in IT spans more than thirty years, marked by travel, reinvention, and a freedom that once seemed out of reach.

In the wake of his mother's awakening, Micah Harold came of age and discovered early that defiance could be a kind of work. In Cedar Grove's rough streets and in the upstairs meetings where ACT UP first gathered, he watched Deborah Allen turn grief into action and silence into movement, and he followed her into it. He had seen this before—the fear, the church-shaped shame, the moment his mother cut off a friend with AIDS because she believed what she had been taught. He also witnessed the after—the apology, the fire, the long nights at folding tables, most of them nearly bare except for the papers Chuck spread out in front of him, covering them in notes.

By his teens, he was hauling signs, raising funds, and standing beside Chuck Selber, Robert Darrow, and Buddy Williamson, absorbing their language of refusal. He remembers pickets outside Congressman Jim McCrery's office, the gallows humor after confrontations, the understanding that rage was not spectacle but fuel.

Today, his tattoo studio, Red Handed Tattoo, on Kings Highway doubles as refuge and rally point, a place where art, empathy, and outrage share the same skin. During the pandemic, he delivered food beneath overpasses, keeping faith with the forgotten. For Micah, rage was never a pose. It was a family current, and he refuses to let it run dry.

Even in the heaviest moments, humor made survival possible. When the room tightened, Buddy Williamson knew how to release it. Born in Shreveport and raised in Stonewall, he learned early that laughter could outwit cruelty. At the Tic-Toc Grill on Line Avenue, his father's small restaurant, he watched the city pass through its doors and learned how conversation could be both shield and stage. The place carried the close, familiar smell of burgers on the grill and fries in the fryer, with the low murmur of customers rising beneath it. The Tic-Toc Grill was a place people returned to—not just for the food, but for what came with it. Its pies were local legend. People came as much for a slice as for a meal, the dessert case drawing regulars and first-timers alike.

By sixteen, he had spotted other gay men in Highland and downtown; by eighteen, slipping into a local bar with a friend named Chuck, he felt the world widen. From those nights to early meetings about AIDS in 1989—invited by Deborah Allen while he was home from USL—irony gave way to action.

He marched with ACT UP to the 1990 CDC protest in Atlanta, where activists demanded women be included in the AIDS definition, founded *Tri-State Tea*, North Louisiana's first gay publication, and later joined the Philadelphia Center as an outreach worker, counselor, and eventually director of direct services, overseeing housing, food, and medication access when few others would.

When spirits flagged, he could steady a room with a story that moved through grief and landed on laughter without denying what it cost. His sharp tongue and big heart were inseparable. Years later, he said, "Even though those were tremendously horrible times, I'm very glad I was a part of it all. It made me the good bitch that I am."

Buddy continues to work in the agricultural field with a national company, spending his time outside of work focused on the life he has built—grounded in love, stability, and the quiet rewards of endurance.

Order didn't come from speeches; it came from someone who showed up every time with the necessary facts. That was Cecil Thad Coburn, the one who opened the bank account, signed the forms no one wanted, and kept a clean ledger of what came in and what could go out.

He grew up in Highland, the kind of boy who rode buses across Shreveport alone to find bookstores, already imagining a life beyond what the city offered. By thirteen, after reading *Memoirs* by Tennessee Williams, he had quietly named himself and decided not to turn back.

College in Monroe, he liked to say, was like setting your watch back ten years, but it also gave him room to breathe and know himself before the shadow of AIDS fell. He worked steadily from seventeen onward, flipping houses and trailer homes, learning how money moved and how quickly it vanished.

When he came home, he built a life on steadiness, working at a local bank in Shreveport, fixing what could be fixed, and finding solid ground in uncertain times. Joe DeSantis pulled him into ACT UP, and he later joked that his first act of rebellion was opening a savings account. Under fluorescent lights, he filled out the paperwork with the name ACT UP stretched across the line in sudden, improbable formality. There was irony in that, but also something steadier taking shape—not just anger, but structure.

He worked doors at Club Euphoria fundraisers, counted the take, and remembered nights that felt more like controlled chaos than the quiet precision of the bank.

"Be sand in the gears," he'd say, "so the machine can't grind you down." Thad remains in Shreveport. Retired. Still standing.

Kenny King found his voice through wit and design, an artist who turned irreverence into resistance. Born in 1965 and raised in a household ruled by discipline and decorum, he learned early how silence could wound and how comedy, aimed well, could expose it. Sobriety brought honesty; activism gave that honesty a job.

A conversation with Gary Cathey at Monty's My Way pulled him into the movement, where his eye for layout, slogan, and spectacle became tools for survival. Onstage, that instinct took fuller form in his drag persona, Kandi D'Taille—a name spelled with precision and worn with pride. At the edge of the stage, he let a pause stretch just long enough to pull the room tight, then broke it with a sharp, deliberate movement that sent the audience into laughter and applause.

As Kandi D'Taille, he wielded glamour like a switchblade, mixing camp, couture, and confrontation into performances that entertained, unsettled, and raised money when both were urgently needed. He wrote press releases, staged fundraisers, and used drag as leverage, winning a Krewe of Apollo contest to reclaim a charity table for the Mercy Center after it had been withdrawn.

His creative fingerprints appeared on campaigns like "Queerness, You're Soaking in It" and "Voodoo You," the latter calling out Louisiana's Department of Health and Hospitals for diverting AIDS funds. When others softened for the sake of paychecks, Kenny refused, choosing candor over comfort.

After ACT UP, he managed the Baja Beach Club with Robert Darrow, donating profits to the Philadelphia Center, and later co-founded the Shreveport AIDS Memorial Foundation, organizing candlelight vigils that turned grief into community.

Now based in San Francisco, he continues to build a life shaped by service. He still carries the lesson forward: art can apply pressure, laughter can be leverage, and service sustains the work.

Not every fight announced itself in sequins and spotlight. Mical DeBrow entered the AIDS crisis from a different angle.

Born in 1954, in Jackson, Mississippi, and raised across small Louisiana towns before claiming Zachary as home, he learned early how to enter a room, read its currents, and steer without spectacle. Leadership was muscle memory—student government, fraternity president, committee chair—structure offering clarity in a region that prized it.

When AIDS began hollowing out gay communities in the early 1980s, he watched friends fall ill while headlines lagged behind reality. Fear moved quickly; facts did not.

Drawn not to confrontation but to infrastructure, he became involved in what would become Greater Louisiana AIDS Defense, working to secure funding, stabilize programs, and meet federal standards. He believed sustainability required discipline rather than disruption.

The divide between that approach and ACT UP's tactics was sharp. Where others saw necessary confrontation, he saw fragile alliances at risk; where activists demanded spectacle, he worried about losing hard-won ground. The tension was personal, not abstract. GLAD believed in education, procedure, and working within the rules; Chuck and ACT UP believed confrontation was sometimes the only thing that moved institutions. Where ACT UP pushed LSU Medical Center and the Northwest Louisiana AIDS Task Force toward drug trials, GLAD saw that kind of pressure as outside its proper scope.

After leaving Shreveport, he continued in HIV education and governance, serving with Project Lazarus and later on the Louisiana Commission on HIV and AIDS. His conviction remained steady: durable change grows from persuasion and structure. After more than twenty years in healthcare technology and the pharmaceutical industry, Mical now lives in Houston, where he consults on the use of artificial intelligence and emerging technologies designed to support—not replace—clinical care.

Carrying the crisis differently still—less strategic than instinctive, less measured than electric, Chad Cromer arrived in Shreveport in 1991 freshly diagnosed and barely twenty, already cycling through addiction, fear, and flight.

Born in Denton, Texas, and hardened early by a home where appearance mattered more than truth, he had been slipping into gay bars by fifteen; by nineteen, he had moved through treatment, the military, and relapse. On June 6, 1990, just days before his twenty-first birthday, he was diagnosed HIV-positive.

Drag houses, sober meetings, and borrowed couches became his first stations of belonging. In those houses, wigs rested on mannequin heads, costumes spilled over chairs, and the air carried hairspray, sweat, and perfume, chaos held together by an unspoken care. It was Kenny King, Robert Darrow, and Kurt Pickett who drew him into ACT UP—not through recruitment speeches, but through friendship. "If they were going, I was going," he later said.

He stood downtown in a suit when Congressman Jim McCrery was confronted, handing out flyers that turned private hypocrisy into public record. At the airport, when President George H. W. Bush arrived, Secret Service tightening the perimeter as umbrellas snapped in the rain and the crowd surged for a better look, Kurt grabbed him and kissed him in full view of the cameras—a flash of unapologetic visibility no one could mistake.

ACT UP did not rescue him from his demons, but it gave his anger direction. The boy who once ran from shame learned to face it without flinching. When the protests quieted, he carried that same defiance forward—not only into the streets, but into the craft that would steady his hands and reshape his future.

Today, Chad lives in Austin, Texas, sober and working in the substance abuse field, helping others find their way through the same darkness he once navigated. That twenty-year-old boy remains with him—grateful to the men and women of Shreveport who planted the seeds of selflessness and purpose he still strives to live by.

Not every activist stood before cameras or chains of police. Some carried the movement in quieter ways, keeping people linked to each other and to care, making sure rage had somewhere to go after the streets emptied. Among them was Tracy Murrell, who entered ACT UP not through spectacle but through the steady work of survival. Born in 1963 in Mobile and raised along the Gulf Coast and abroad in a military family, she came to Shreveport shaped by resilience and a belief in education as repair.

After college, she worked with the YMCA in Shreveport, where she saw firsthand how limited HIV outreach services truly were. In response, she founded the Health and AIDS Network Database (H.A.N.D.), using Ryan White funding to expand testing, education, and prevention into small towns across North Louisiana—places like Minden, Ruston, and rural parishes where services were scarce, building routes of care where shame had made roads impassable. The towns she entered were often quiet in a way that settled deep—empty clinics, long stretches of road, and conversations kept polite enough to avoid naming what was actually happening. She set up in borrowed spaces, making something visible in places where it had been left unspoken.

At her first AIDS coalition meeting, silence filled the room until Chuck Selber stood and applauded, beginning a friendship that drew her into ACT UP's core. She taught safer sex with humor and clarity, spoke in churches and community halls where few dared, and carried dignity into rooms where others saw only fear.

When the deaths came—Chuck Selber, Anthony Hill, and so many others—she carried on until grief demanded rest. In time, she moved to

Atlanta to work in the industry, and later turned to art, painting the Black female form in luminous blues, insisting on humanity before assumption.

Her life remains proof that activism can be quiet and still be fierce.

That same refusal to play small traveled far beyond Shreveport. At the 1990 CDC protest in Atlanta, Jason "J" Bratlie stood shoulder to shoulder with women demanding their illnesses be named in the AIDS definition. Raised in a conservative Louisiana home, he learned early to question authority; while other kids traded baseball cards, he read *Civil Disobedience* and imagined how to build a fairer world. An Eagle Scout as a teenager, he organized repairs for families in need, already understanding that service could be its own kind of rebellion.

Restless with pretense and allergic to hypocrisy, he carried that instinct into activism, marching against David Duke, protesting the Gulf War, then joining ACT UP Shreveport. At the CDC protest in Atlanta, when the giant sign cracked and a letter fell free, he picked up the "F" and carried it back home to Natchitoches, a small physical reminder of a moment when anger forced attention.

He did not stay in ACT UP for the long haul, but the lesson stayed with him. Years later, when Crohn's disease nearly took his life, he recognized the same fault lines—fear, neglect, and systems that decide whose pain counts. He survived again, still loud, still holding the "F."

Jason now teaches music privately—working with students in piano, guitar, and voice—and continues to perform as a member of the touring band Dirtfoot. Music remains both his craft and his way of staying connected—to people, to place, and to the creative life that shaped him.

Back in Louisiana, others carried the fight into more formal rooms. Dr. Marcus Spurlock—known to many simply as Marc—did it with a steady voice and a white coat that opened doors most activists could only pound on.

Born in 1957 at Schumpert Sanitarium and raised in North Shreveport, he excelled early—scholarship student, clarinetist, early admit to LSU's medical school—before entering the Air Force as a young physician during the early years of the AIDS crisis. There, he encountered a dying soldier with symptoms few dared to name. When he pursued the truth, his career was quietly dismantled, his loyalty questioned, and his home searched while he was away. They found almost nothing—only a postcard from a friend playful enough to be read as evidence by people determined to find some. Compassion, he learned, carried consequences.

Returning home, he built a family practice and, pushed by patients to learn, trained to treat HIV directly when few local doctors would. He co-founded the Philadelphia Center, fought Baton Rouge to keep Ryan White funds in North Louisiana, and stood beside Robert Darrow in their "good-cop, bad-cop" dynamic that forced the state to pay attention.

His care extended beyond policy and protocol; patients trusted him because he spoke to them as equals, not cases. Even after protests quieted, he kept working the same pressure points—in clinics, boardrooms, and committee meetings—advocating for those the system preferred not to see.

Yeona DaCosta-Auld entered those same hospital corridors from a different direction. Where Marc carried authority into boardrooms, Yeona carried presence into rooms where authority often failed.

Her path to Shreveport crossed continents—born in Nairobi, raised in Goa, trained by Irish nuns in Bangalore, seasoned in psychiatric wards in Bahrain—before serendipity placed her at Schumpert Medical Center, one of the primary hospitals serving Shreveport, in 1985. When told there was no opening in psychiatry, she asked simply to be assigned "where it was busy" and was sent to Nine Tower, the medical unit that would become the city's de facto AIDS ward. It carried a hush beyond ordinary hospital quiet, with closed doors, lowered voices, and a stillness that made each room feel larger than the space itself.

Working the 3–11 shift and rising quickly to charge nurse, she cared for young men nearing the end of their lives. In a hospital climate thick with fear, she listened closely as Marc explained what infection control required. For procedures, she wore the gown and shield. For greetings, for conversation, for a hand resting on a shoulder, she stepped inside without the barrier.

Many patients had no one left willing to sit beside them. She made a private vow that, if she could help it, they would not die alone.

As the first Indian nurse at Schumpert, she absorbed the city's awkward racial categories with steady grace, answering gently and returning to her work. She never called herself brave. She called herself a nurse. In rooms where stigma tried to dictate distance, her decision to remain present altered the air itself.

Yeona now serves as Clinical Administrator for Northwest Louisiana Nephrology, following more than two decades in clinical research in nephrology. Though her role has shifted, her commitment to patient care has not. She still sees nursing as both calling and practice—grounded in the same instinct to care that defined her work from the beginning.

Some nights sagged under grief, and James Smith carried what others could not.

Born the youngest of six in Somerville, Tennessee, he was raised between hymnals and hard work, a preacher's son who learned early that discipline and tenderness were not opposites. In a town of one church and six houses, his father served as principal, pastor, and bus driver, and James learned to measure his days by sermons and back roads.

Sensitive and restless, drawn more to flowers than tools, he found his calling first in service—working with people with disabilities before training as a nurse. Nursing became his pulpit. He brought charts instead of sermons, steadiness instead of doctrine, and an unflinching belief that care itself could be a form of resistance.

When HIV entered his own life, he met it without pretense, loving Kurt Pickett through diagnosis, grief, and defiance. It was Marc who steered him toward Robert Darrow and ACT UP, where James found rage and refuge in equal measure.

He forged friendships that deepened into purpose, most profoundly with Chuck Selber. James sang in a Christmas cantata, unaware until it ended that Chuck had died. When a friend told him afterward, the news overtook him. The music changed him.

From that night forward, every act of care became a memorial. He carried that calling into Mercy Center, the Philadelphia Center, and later as president of Access Care Coastal Texas, reminding others that compassion, practiced faithfully and without flinching, is still one of the bravest ways to fight.

Mark Anthony Lindsey made his stand in sickrooms and spotlight alike. Born under Shreveport's August heat, he found his people early— drag bars, backlots, and makeshift families that loved without apology.

Known to many as Marquita, his quick-witted drag persona at Central Station, he became a familiar presence behind the bar and under the lights, adored by regulars who still call him by that name.

When hospitals refused to touch the dying, Mark Anthony and Deborah Allen walked in anyway and stayed for hours because they were often the only caregivers those patients had. While hospital staff kept their distance, they acted as lay nurses, bringing presence where fear had left abandonment. He didn't make his case in the streets with a bullhorn.

He sang through heartbreak, two or three numbers a night at Bubba's, raising money for rent, medicine, and dignified burials.

Later, at the Nelson-Tebedo Clinic in Dallas, he turned that same steadiness into precision, running its dental program for fifteen years and insisting that care required both skill and tenderness.

"Education, education, education," he said, a mantra against complacency. Now living on his family's land near Alexandria, still fighting stage 4 cancer, he carries on with humor, faith, and Barkley the corgi at his heels.

For Mark Anthony, rage was never only a march. It remains part of how he lives. Sometimes it was eyeliner in the ER—love refusing to leave.

Mark Anthony remains active with the Philadelphia Center, supporting awareness and fundraising efforts. He continues to find joy in music, playing piano daily, singing in his church choir, and sharing his home with his dog Barkley and his three roosters—Hudson, Duke, and Baby. His years of performance and community presence remain part of the foundation he carries forward.

Art spoke when chants could not, and Richard Kightlinger carried that truth on canvas. Born in Shreveport in 1962, the youngest in his family, he grew up bullied for his softness and for the friends he refused to abandon, especially Black classmates in a city still sorting itself by color. Long before he knew the word "activist," he understood its cost.

Against his father's wishes, who imagined medicine or biology, he chose paint over predictability, declaring independence through color and form. At LSU, he experimented with cardboard, wood, newspaper, even porcelain plates, breaking the frame as if the frame itself were the problem.

By the time AIDS began hollowing out his generation, he already understood what it meant to live on the margins. With ACT UP Shreveport, he showed up where silence needed breaking: at the Pickle Barrel protest, at Centenary's candlelight vigils, at Broadmoor Baptist Church beside Chuck Selber, bearing a pink triangle during a Holocaust memorial few wanted to remember. At first, some in the crowd seemed unsure whether the interruption was part of the program. Once they understood it was protest, many tried to look away. He painted, he marched, he grieved.

To Richard, art and activism were never separate. They were survival and confession, a way of saying: I am here.

Richard lives in Washington, D.C., where he works as an artist and part-time teacher. His work continues to explore mixed media—cardboard, collage, wood—layered forms that reflect both memory and resistance. He remains active in advocacy, continuing the work both artistically and socially.

If Richard gave resistance color, Bryan Sullivan gave it steadiness. He came from pine trees and red clay—Sibley, Louisiana—where silence was taught before speech and conformity was a kind of currency.

Born in 1967, the youngest of three boys raised in a trailer deep in the woods, he learned early how small towns measure difference. The spotlight found him anyway—school plays, then Mr. Sibley High School, Class of 1985—proof that presence could outshine caution.

Beauty school gave him craft; a July 4 night in 1986, stepping into a gay bar with friends, gave him language. It carried through beauty school, across Robert Darrow's backyard pool, and into ACT UP meetings at Shoney's restaurant in Shreveport, where he found the people who made sense of him. In the back room, coffee cups sat among flyers and scribbled notes while voices rose, quieted, and rose again, the restaurant hum continuing just beyond the walls.

He wasn't always at the microphone, but he was there—printing shirts, designing posters, holding the line when exhaustion threatened to break the circle. At Broadmoor Baptist, he stood with other ACT UP members as Chuck Selber raised a pink triangle in protest, and years later, he stood graveside in Boston for Kurt Pickett.

Those two moments, bound by love and defiance, shaped his faith in visibility. When ACT UP's urgency shifted into service, Bryan carried it forward—into Mardi Gras krewes, PTA boards, and eventually PACE, where he led Shreveport's first LGBTQ+ film festival and helped spark another generation's awakening.

Through every incarnation, his message stayed the same: fear is loud, but courage lasts longer.

Bryan and his partner of more than two decades, James, are raising their teenage nephew while building a life rooted in both family and community. He now owns a multi-location salon company, creating opportunities for young artists while continuing his work in the community. His work extends into the broader community through service, including his role on the board of the Red River Revel Arts Festival.

Dave Herrell's defiance began with a single word: yes. Born in 1971 on Florida's Space Coast and raised in Louisiana's military hush, he learned early that honesty could be costly.

By his teens, he had already come out—first as bisexual, then as gay—refusing to disappear into the silence expected of small-town boys. At Northwestern State University, he helped found the first recognized queer student group, organizing forums and marches that said what classrooms and pulpits would not.

His path led to ACT UP Shreveport, where he met Alana Oldham and Chuck Selber, carrying North Louisiana's refusal onto the national stage. At the 1990 CDC protest in Atlanta, he stood in the downpour as police moved through the crowd in gloves and rain gear, arresting protesters demanding women be included in the AIDS definition. Activists staged die-ins on the pavement, forcing grief into public view, and the pressure they sustained helped push the CDC, by 1993, to widen the definition at last.

He brought that spirit home, blanketing his campus with Silence = Death stickers, the now-iconic symbol of AIDS activism, that still whisper from old walls.

Years later, his activism continues in quieter ways—in classrooms, in conversations, in the unbroken thread between truth and visibility. His life remains proof that saying yes to yourself is its own kind of revolution.

The fire Chuck carried was later preserved on film by those who refused to let it die. Raydra Hall hadn't marched with ACT UP, but she found her way into its aftermath through light, sound, and story.

Born in Baton Rouge in 1974 and raised among East Texas pines and North Louisiana soil, she learned early that love meant showing up. A photographer turned graphic designer turned filmmaker, she first carried a camera in her teens, chasing weddings, senior portraits, and live bands, discovering that framing was its own form of truth-telling. One early shoot took place in a cemetery with her younger sister, the image already hinting at her instinct for the charged and the unexpected.

Training in commercial photography in Atlanta sharpened her eye; later studies in graphic and web design sharpened her voice. At the Betty and Leonard Phillips Deaf Action Center, where she served for nearly twelve years, she developed the video and editing skills that would become central to her storytelling.

In 2012, she partnered with David Hylan to co-direct *Small Town*

Rage: Fighting Back in the Deep South, a documentary preserving the story of ACT UP Shreveport, turning silence into testimony. Beyond the screen, she built community—founding Free Mom Hugs–Shreveport, offering embrace where rejection once stood; serving within PACE; raising two sons, both members of the LGBTQ+ community, teaching them that visibility is not a flaw but a lineage.

The stories she helped preserve were not distant histories. They belonged to people still shaping the city in quieter ways.

That same defiance shaped Dr. David Hylan's path. Born in 1959, on an Air Force base in Dover, Delaware, he grew up under discipline and doctrine, eventually becoming the eldest son of a Southern Baptist minister in a world where faith and politics braided tightly together.

In a city that preferred closets sealed tight, he learned early how silence could wound and how truth, once spoken, could heal. He married, became a father of three, and followed every rule expected of him, even as the truth flickered beneath the surface.

For decades, he translated the world through other people's voices as a nationally certified sign-language interpreter, standing between silence and meaning long before finding the courage to interpret his own life aloud. The work often placed him inside the most intimate moments of other people's lives—delivering news of sudden death, terminal illness, and irreversible loss with nowhere to hide from the human cost of words.

He served for thirty-eight years as executive director of the Betty and Leonard Phillips Deaf Action Center, retiring after nearly four decades of advocacy and leadership.

When he finally came out, he lost family, friends, and colleagues—but gained himself. From that honesty came PACE, People Acting for Change and Equality, which he co-founded in 2004 with Dr. Adrienne Critcher and Dr. Robert Darrow. He wrote its bylaws like scaffolding, built with care and conviction, and later helped pass Shreveport's Fairness Ordinance, shifting the city's civic weather toward inclusion.

Through film he preserved what time might erase, co-directing *Small Town Rage: Fighting Back in the Deep South* with Raydra Hall and *CLOSET2PRIDE* with Dr. Robert Darrow. His activism no longer depended on public confrontation; it lived in service, in story, in steady persistence.

Now living on an island in Mexico with his husband, Troy Hylan, he carries the work forward with quieter tools and the same certainty: rage, tempered by love, can rebuild what fear once tried to destroy.

Not every act of defiance came with a bullhorn. Sometimes it looked like a ride across town, a meal on a plate, a stack of flyers run off after midnight, or groceries carried to a front door with a few careful words about testing, treatment, and not being alone. Their voices were different. Their methods often clashed. But they stayed, and because they stayed, something held. Out of ACT UP's fire came something that could endure beyond protest alone—what had been urgency began to take form; what had been reaction became structure.

The work did not end. It rooted itself, built itself, and opened its doors to those who needed it most—taking shape inside the Philadelphia Center, where it would hold.

CHAPTER 8
THE PHILADELPHIA CENTER

"ACT UP forced the door open. The Philadelphia Center made sure someone was waiting on the other side."
> —Gary Cathey, founding member of ACT UP Shreveport

There are cities where epidemics are remembered in numbers. Shreveport is not one of them. Here, the early years of AIDS were tallied in hospital wards, in midnight phone calls, and in funerals that multiplied faster than anyone could keep pace.

By the late 1980s, pretense had fallen away. At LSU Medical Center, the problem was not only virology but culture. AIDS patients at LSU Medical Center were primarily treated in the Medical Intensive Care Unit (MICU), where the most critical cases were managed. The doors of patients with AIDS bore yellow-and-black biohazard signs—a message clear enough: danger before dignity, fear before care. LSUMC administrators debated installing exhaust fans to carry patients' breath out of buildings, and staff sometimes slid food trays across floors rather than enter the room. Others, paid in little more than conscience, crossed that line and sat with patients whose hands had grown light as a feather.

The rooms carried their own weather. Latex snapped at the wrists, gowns rustled like paper, and the smell—bleach layered over something metallic and human—never quite left. Charts hung at the foot of the bed, clipped and re-clipped, as if order could be imposed through paper. Some nurses learned to read a room before stepping inside: whether there would be anger, silence, or the kind of quiet that meant the end was near. Others kept their distance, letting protocol stand in for presence. Families passed those doors and felt the weight of what the signs implied. In those same months, anger began to organize into what would, in December 1989, take the name ACT UP Shreveport.

Inside that same atmosphere, where policy often outweighed medicine, the idea of a different kind of institution began to form. Protest had already done its job: it broke the silence. ACT UP Shreveport stormed meetings, challenged hospital leadership, and demanded an end to practices that treated patients as contagion. Its members pressed for clinical trials to reach the region, for doctors to stop hiding behind euphemisms, and for the press to print the word AIDS without apology. And still, after the chanting and the leaflets and the shaking doors, a harder question remained: protest had forced action—but what waited beyond that breach? Where would you send the man who had just been told he was positive, whose job would not keep him, whose church would not bless him, whose family did not answer the phone? Shreveport needed something lasting—not just a slogan or a vigil, but a place that made survival possible. The answer came slowly, then all at once. It did not arrive fully formed. It began as conversations that lingered after meetings, as notes scribbled in margins, as the same question asked again: what happens after the protest ends? People who had learned to organize anger now had to organize care. The shift was not immediate. It required a different kind of endurance—the patience to build something that would still be standing after the urgency of the moment had passed.

What many outside the movement did not see was that the Philadelphia Center was not separate from ACT UP's story—it was its continuation. The same people who had marched, chained themselves to doors, and demanded accountability now learned the language of grants, budgets, and case management. Rage did not disappear; it changed posture. Civil disobedience gave way to daily administration. Protest became paperwork. The goal remained the same: keep people alive.

The Philadelphia Center, in practice, was not born of optimism;

it was assembled out of scarcity and refusal. In 1990, after Dr. Marcus Spurlock secured Ryan White funding for direct services in Shreveport, the organization formally began. Marc chose the name for its plain meaning—"the city of brotherly love"—a marker of brothers helping brothers when the burden fell hardest on gay men. Marc understood the math: without insurance, people would die waiting for care. "One of the reasons we established the Center was to help those without insurance get adequate medical care," he said. That aim was not charity; it was strategy—bringing patients into care earlier—evaluated at the Viral Disease Clinic at LSU Medical Center, given the right drugs, supported by a social worker—so the hospital could become a last resort rather than the only destination.

Marc's conviction became structure. He wrote the region's first successful Ryan White grant for direct services from his own patients' files and the numbers no one else wanted to count. He worked late, stitching statistics to stories, and sent the application. When the award came through, the scale of possibility changed. The letter itself was unremarkable—typed, formal, easy to miss. But once opened, it altered the trajectory of everything that followed. It meant salaries instead of stipends, appointments instead of guesswork, continuity instead of improvisation. It meant that the work could extend beyond whoever happened to show up that day and become something that could be counted on.

The Philadelphia Center moved from a borrowed desk to an organization that could hire staff, pay rent, build programs, and answer the phone every time it rang. The phone became its own kind of barometer. Some days it rang without pause—questions, crises, referrals stacked one on top of another. Other days it went quiet long enough to make everyone uneasy, as if silence itself signaled something worse. Staff learned to listen not just to what was said, but to what wasn't: hesitation, confusion, the moment before someone admitted they had run out of medication or nowhere left to go. The Center could do more than comfort; it could intervene.

One of the first changes came through housing. Mercy Center opened its doors in September 1989, just before the Philadelphia Center formally took shape. It grew out of the Northwest Louisiana AIDS Task Force, which had identified housing as its most urgent priority. The Catholic Diocese of Shreveport offered a recently donated home from

　　　　　　　　　DR. DAVID W. HYLAN

the Thomas family, with Monsignor Murray Clayton making clear that people living with HIV would not die abandoned by family or turned away by nursing homes.

Social workers Sam Lucero and Chris Miciotto helped draft the first house policies and prepare Mercy Center for residents. In December 1990, the Sisters of Charity of the Incarnate Word / Schumpert Medical Center assumed operations and expanded capacity by renovating an adjacent property, giving the project institutional stability and daily care.

A formal letter from Schumpert Medical Center in January 1993 documented the transfer of Mercy Center's administration and affirmed continued partnership with the Philadelphia Center, marking Mercy Center's integration into the region's growing network of HIV care. It became a place where people could live with dignity instead of dying alone. Mornings settled into routine. Coffee brewed early, strong and constant. A radio played softly somewhere down the hall. Residents moved slowly at first, then with more certainty, learning the rhythms of shared space—when the shower was free, who liked the window open, which chair belonged to whom. There were arguments, too, over small things that only mattered because people were still there to argue about them. The Center carried that mission forward, ensuring the program endured beyond its hospital beginnings. Hallways smelled of coffee and institutional cleaner. On good afternoons, someone set out plants on the stoop and spoke to them as if coaxing roots was a kind of prayer.

Those first months after the Center was awarded the federal Ryan White grant were held together with tape and grit. With little more than that first grant and about $5,000 in cash, the Center ran on borrowed desks and volunteer stamina. Marc remembered the pharmacy shelves—half-empty, a few bottles of AZT, trimethoprim-sulfamethoxazole for opportunistic infections, and sample blister packs stacked in rows. "We filled the clinic with prescriptions," he said. Donations trickled in, then quickened. A local pharmacist agreed to float inventory until reimbursement came. The Viral Disease Clinic at LSUMC became a partner rather than an obstacle: physicians coordinated refills, nurses called when side effects toppled patients, and case managers translated medical language into instructions people could follow. In a city where hospitals had often looked away, there was now a place where someone looked back—with compassion, and with action.

The Center's design was intentional: medicine alone couldn't heal what AIDS had broken. The staff built a bridge between the exam room and the rest of a person's life. That bridge was not abstract. It was built from appointments kept and calls returned, from forms completed correctly the first time, from showing up when a system expected absence. It required persistence more than inspiration. Each small success—a benefit approved, a prescription filled, a landlord persuaded— extended the span just a little further. Case managers kept calendars, not just charts. They learned bus routes and kept food vouchers in their desk drawers. They practiced difficult conversations with clients—how to tell a mother, a boss, how to request a leave of absence without revealing more than the law required. The Buddy Program paired clients with volunteers who could drive at dawn to lab draws and sit up late when fever returned. In kitchens and front rooms across the city, buddies pressed pills into hands, made soup, and stayed. The Center's food pantry stocked peanut butter, rice, and shelf-stable soups, often donated by parish churches that would not yet say the word AIDS from the pulpit but could not ignore the need.

Growth arrived quickly, heavy and hard to contain. The small office on Margaret Place filled, then overflowed. Intake forms multiplied in manila folders. Volunteers stepped in where they could: one created a system with color-coded tabs; another designed a flyer for anonymous testing and convinced a bar along Texas Street to post it in the bathroom. Crisis work expanded, and fundraising followed. The Strand Theatre— an ornate 1920s movie palace with a sweeping marquee on Louisiana Avenue and a chandeliered auditorium that rises in tiers of red velvet and gold—opened its doors for the annual Auction Against AIDS, bringing the city together under stage lights instead of hospital fluorescents. Artists donated canvases and ceramics for bidding, but ARTport, a fundraising auction held inside a hangar at Shreveport Regional Airport, stood apart—where art met runway. Organizers mailed ceramic tile kits to well-known celebrities across the country. The decorated tiles came back signed, glazed, and ready for auction. People crowded around them, drawn as much to the names as the work itself. The proceeds returned home to fund care at the Philadelphia Center.

For one evening, talk turned from fear to generosity. People dressed for those nights. Jackets pressed, dresses chosen with care. The rituals mattered as much as the money raised. For a few hours, the city practiced a different version of itself—one where attendance signaled not distance but involvement. Conversations that would not happen elsewhere unfolded easily under stage lights, as if proximity made honesty possible. Envelopes arrived with careful handwriting in the corner—some with five-dollar bills, others with checks that carried the weight of a mortgage payment. And then, in a city that specialized in withholding welcome, something rare took shape. The Victorian mansion that housed the Florentine Club—a former supper club where, in the 1950s, Shreveport's social elite gathered beneath low chandeliers for long dinners, clinking glasses, and the quiet performance of status—stood wood-framed and worn but still standing. Its rooms, once filled with laughter and perfume and the choreography of fine dining, were donated by its owner to become the home of the Philadelphia Center.

For a moment, it felt like an answer—not imagined, not promised, but held. Walls where there had only been barriers. A place that could be pointed to, stepped into, claimed. In a city that had so often said no, it felt like something solid enough to believe in.

But the structure had already begun to give way. Termites had worked through the wood long before the deed changed hands, hollowing it from the inside out. Time had done the rest. Contractors walked through, measuring what hope had briefly claimed, and the number they carried back was staggering—more than a million dollars to make it safe and usable.

A million dollars might as well have been the moon.

What had felt like arrival shifted into something more uncertain. The building remained, but it could not hold what people needed. What had been offered was real, but not yet enough to hold. Still, people walked through it one more time before letting it go. They stood in doorways and tried to imagine desks, waiting rooms, a place where someone could sit without being turned away. The vision lingered longer than the structure could sustain. When they left, they carried that image with them, knowing the building had failed but the need had not.

Meanwhile, beyond that failed promise, the city learned new rituals. On World AIDS Day, observed each year on December 1, the Texas Street Bridge in downtown Shreveport went dark, turning the skyline into a question. Candlelight vigils gathered at Centenary College's Hargrove Memorial Amphitheater—known simply as "the Shell," a natural, bowl-shaped outdoor stage carved into the campus, where stone seating curves around a central platform beneath open sky, a place long used for Easter sunrise services, concerts, and moments of communal reflection—where names were spoken aloud into the night air. It was there, in February 1992, that the AIDS Memorial Quilt unfurled across that same stage. Volunteers, including Gary Cathey and his husband Justin Normand, lifted panels into the open sky. Chuck Selber's name joined thousands. Names once whispered behind closed doors and in hospital rooms now filled public space. Grief had moved outdoors. And once a city speaks its dead aloud, it becomes harder to pretend the living do not need care.

The political weather did not always favor compassion. In the early 1990s, Louisiana Governor Buddy Roemer—then midway through a single, reform-minded term—scrambled to locate funding for AIDS clinics. Political promises leapt ahead of appropriations; in the parishes around Shreveport, the result was delay in funding. Editorials urged the city to measure itself not by fear but by care. ACT UP did what it had always done: forced the subject. Demonstrations outside hospital boardrooms and city offices demanded money, trials, and humanity. The Philadelphia Center took that fury and translated it into paperwork, casework, and continuity. Staffed in its earliest days by people from the same circle who had marched, leafleted, and organized, the movement's energy shifted into something more durable. The noise of protest gave way to client intake forms, yet the urgency remained. Protest moved the needle, and the Center kept it from slipping back.

But the fight over information did not end in hospitals or funding debates. It moved into classrooms.

Across Caddo Parish, another message was taking hold. Since the mid-1980s, the school district had relied on *Sex Respect: The Option of True Sexual Freedom*, an abstinence-only curriculum that taught students to "just say no" to sex—framing restraint as morality, and morality as protection. It spoke of self-control, of waiting, of consequences. It did not speak, with any clarity, about condoms.

Among those pushing back, Robert Darrow of The Philadelphia Center became one of the most vocal critics of the curriculum, challenging what he saw as misinformation presented as moral authority. He pointed to a line from the textbook itself—"Pet your dog, not your date"—a phrase that reduced a public health crisis to slogans while sidestepping the realities young people were already facing.

For ACT UP Shreveport, this was not a philosophical disagreement. It was a matter of survival.

Members showed up in force—at school board meetings, public

                              DR. DAVID W. HYLAN

forums, and community gatherings—filling rooms, lining walls, stepping to microphones one after another. They spoke plainly and repeatedly, insisting that prevention required truth. They argued that abstinence, presented as the only answer, was not only unrealistic but irresponsible in a world where teenagers were already making decisions about sex. They pointed to what was already visible: rising rates of sexually transmitted infections among young people, evidence that abstinence-only messaging was not preventing risk but obscuring it. To them, withholding information was not caution. It was dangerous. It meant that those defending the curriculum were not protecting young people, but gambling with their lives.

Robert carried that same urgency beyond the room. In the pages of *The Shreveport Times*, he warned with blunt clarity: "AIDS isn't going away; our children are left to educate themselves."

Parents across Shreveport, led by activists including Mary Ellen Hoffman, began to push back. The resistance came at a cost. Hoffman was labeled a heathen, a "lesbian lover," her credibility attacked in the language of the very culture she was challenging. But the objections held. The curriculum, they argued, was medically inaccurate, rooted in religious ideology, and dangerously incomplete in the middle of a public health crisis.

By the early 1990s, the fight had moved from meeting rooms to the courts. ACT UP Shreveport stood with the parents, supporting the lawsuit and providing whatever help the effort required—public pressure, presence, and persistence. In March 1993, a Louisiana state judge ruled against the program, finding that Sex Respect contained medical inaccuracies and impermissible religious content. The legal challenge reinforced the ruling, targeting the curriculum's claims and its place in public education.

The curriculum had promised protection through absence. What it delivered was silence. ACT UP had always known the cost of that— because the consequences did not stay in classrooms or courtrooms. They arrived elsewhere, quietly and without interruption.

Inside hospital rooms, where the consequences never paused, Yeona's rounds continued, steady against the city's denial. She watched families teach themselves new kinds of courage. A sister wiped fever from a brow with the hem of her dress because no nurse answered the call button. A father whispered prayers he had never learned to say aloud. In rooms without kin, Yeona's voice and the scratch of her pen on a chart became proof that someone's life mattered. And now, at the edge of those rooms, another presence began to appear—not a protest line, not a camera, but a case manager with a list: a Medicaid hearing, a Social Security application awaiting signatures, a bag of groceries, a ride to the clinic, a support-group meeting. This was the Philadelphia Center arriving as it always did—one life at a time. Sometimes they met at the threshold—Yeona finishing her rounds, a case manager arriving with paperwork and a plan. One had witnessed the decline; the other carried the next step. Between them, something shifted. Care no longer ended at the hospital door. It continued outward, into whatever came next.

By 1994, as that work continued, another turn came. Marc recognized that the Center's expanding mission required dedicated leadership and helped recruit Robert Darrow, whose roots in ACT UP grounded the role, as its first executive director, transforming the operation from a volunteer-driven effort into a sustainable institution. Robert shaped the Center's stability and growth, then continued to serve on the board, preserving its history and guiding policy. The building that houses the Center now bears his name—the Robert K. Darrow Building. Marc remained a steady public voice and board leader, widening the Center's reach and ensuring continuity. The Buddy Program continued matching volunteers with clients, anonymous testing continued in rooms that barely contained their own furniture, and the Strand Theatre's stage filled again for an auction as Centenary's amphitheater flickered with candles. A different kind of stamina set in—that stubborn, unglamorous endurance that marks institutions made by hand.

That same endurance shaped how the Philadelphia Center approached care. It did not limit itself to one kind of care. Prevention moved wherever doors would open—or stay open long enough. Outreach workers distributed condoms in bars, beauty and barber shops, tucked pamphlets under windshield wipers at night, and talked with teenagers who couldn't ask their questions anywhere else. When schools closed their doors, the Center stood in parking lots; when churches declined a microphone, the Center sat on porches and spoke with uncles and aunties after services. Testing days took place in community centers with coffee and boxes of Southern Maid Donuts to humanize the needle. It didn't preach that prevention erased sin—it taught that prevention saved lives.

Residents learned each other's rhythms, traded rides, and monitored fevers with practiced calm. Nearly two decades later, in 2011, Bryan House, an expansion of Mercy Center's housing program, extended that vision. Located in Shreveport's historic Ledbetter Heights—named for blues musician Huddie "Lead Belly" Ledbetter and once known for its red-light corridor of brothels and bars along Fannin Street—it added independent-living apartments that allowed residents to measure survival not just in days but in calendars—the kind hung on a refrigerator with a magnet, marking rent due dates, birthdays, and doctor visits they intended to keep. For many, Mercy Center became what LSU Medical Center never could—a place where care was not triage but tenure.

The Center's staff were part social worker, part navigator, part witness. They learned which supervisors answered before lunch and which pharmacists would call back. They knew how to laugh when a bureaucratic letter used the wrong name and when to walk a client into an office and wait until someone finally listened. They tracked side effects, reminded people to eat with their pills, and taught persistence— the kind with a soft voice and a sharp pencil. Their desks were layered with sticky notes and photographs: a birthday cake, a porch ringed with folding chairs, a hospital room with a banner taped above the bed. They kept black clothes for funerals and clean shirts for first days at jobs that still asked too many questions.

The Philadelphia Center's public face stayed plainly visible. City proclamations in Shreveport marked World AIDS Day, and the downtown Texas Street Bridge went dark again and again. Mayors came to microphones and spoke the same careful words, each time with more ease. Staff moved among those ceremonies, building the set so the town could say what it needed to say. By December 2009, Shreveport City Hall began to reflect the Center's language—practical, specific, insistent on dignity—when Mayor Cedric Glover signed an executive order adding sexual orientation, gender identity, and disability to city-employee protections, paired with a council resolution to strengthen nondiscrimination policy. Over time, the shape of grief changed. At first it was all endings; then, as medical treatments improved, it became endurance that demanded discipline. Protease inhibitors and combination therapies offered years, and years brought new questions: How do you stay on the drug regimen when your stomach flips every morning? How do you love again? How do you explain yourself to a boss who still thinks AIDS is just a headline from somewhere else? The Center adjusted—adding adherence counseling and employment support, and making space for what survival required.

The Center's collaborations expanded. Physicians at Schumpert Medical Center and LSUMC referred patients with new steadiness. Social workers learned to start sentences with what was possible instead of what was not. The Catholic Diocese's hospital presence, through Schumpert Medical Center, continued to cooperate, making additional space available that allowed the Philadelphia Center to expand its reach. Pastors called for advice on how to preach without injuring; teachers asked for handouts that wouldn't get them called into a principal's office. In the public square, the tone began to shift. If you traced those calls on a map, the lines would have crossed the Red River and both sides of Texas Street, stretched over Allendale and Queensborough neighborhoods, touched the suburbs, and slipped out along two-lane roads into parishes where whispers still covered the truth. The Center became part of Shreveport's civic fabric.

In the files, that civic fabric becomes visible—names of donors whose checks spanned years. Some were businesses—the Strand Theatre, which made a stage for generosity; a downtown gallery that kept a sign in the window for a month because the owner's brother had died and she was tired of explaining why. Others were individuals—five-dollar bills scotch-taped to index cards, payroll-deduction slips from hospital workers who couldn't change policy but could add to someone's medication co-pay. Beyond the ledgers, the city's social pages recorded the same network— the people who once organized benefits now gathering at a restaurant to toast a friend's engagement. The benefit became its own kind of holiday— loud, imperfect, and enough.

There were years when the Center felt alone. A pastor condemned safer-sex education from a pulpit. A landlord evicted a tenant after finding pill bottles in a trash bag. A school board canceled an education session because someone said the word condom twice. The Center endured those seasons by narrowing its focus—the next client, the next intake, the next refill, the next meeting with a state office. But there were also years when the Center felt carried—by a surprise grant, by a mayor who showed up unannounced at a vigil and stayed in the cold, by a high school senior who raised money selling cookies because her uncle, who was living with AIDS, had once taught her how to change a tire. The Center learned that hope sometimes arrives in practical ways.

What did it add up to? Ask the people who walked through the door. A man from Bossier whose family would not answer his calls sat with a counselor and learned how to set an alarm to take his pills. A woman from the Cedar Grove neighborhood bought an extra bus pass so the next person who came in wouldn't be stranded. A teenager who had broken out in hives after his first regimen sat in a chair and cried until the rash faded and he could imagine kissing someone again. A mother from Blanchard dropped off a casserole with no note attached. None of those moments made the paper. All of them made the Center into a house rather than a hallway.

In those same early years, help often traveled by instinct before it traveled by policy. One evening, when Jamie Morris was serving as volunteer coordinator for the Philadelphia Center, balancing college classes with a part-time bartending shift at TS Station, a local bar and restaurant, his mother, Nancy Morris Cook, answered a late-night phone call at home. A young man's voice trembled on the other end of the line. He asked for Jamie. He had used his last quarter to make the call and was standing at a pay phone with nowhere else to go.

Jamie's mother took down the number from the phone booth and promised that someone would call him back within minutes. She reached Jamie at work and said the caller sounded frightened. By the next day, she would learn why. The young man, still a teenager, had told his parents he was gay and HIV-positive. His father handed him a single quarter and told him to leave.

Jamie did not wait for office hours or committee approval. He sent a taxi to pick the teenager up and bring him to TS Station. What happened after that unfolded quietly, without press or proclamation—only friends gathering around someone who had just been cast out. By the time Jamie returned home the following day, the young man had an apartment and food in the cabinets. No forms were filed that night. No policy guided what happened. It moved through instinct, through a network that existed because people had already decided no one would be left alone if they could help it. By morning, what had begun as a crisis had been absorbed into something steadier—a system built not from design, but from response.

Stories like that rarely make archives. But they were not rare. In cities without Marcus Spurlock, Robert Darrow, or Chuck Selber willing to fight for infrastructure, young people like him often disappeared into statistics. In Shreveport, because the Philadelphia Center existed, and because people inside it answered the phone, one terrified teenager did not.

Marc's original vision held in moments like that. He said the Center must be a bridge. On one side stood the Viral Disease Clinic—the wards, the language of T-cells and viral loads, the acronyms and the side effects. On the other stood jobs and porches and funerals and birthdays and arguments over which channel to watch in the common room. That crossing was not figurative; it was a set of practices: a case manager calling in the morning, a pharmacy bag with the right name, a bus timetable folded into a wallet, a conversation with a landlord, a call to a pastor willing to sit with a mother who was terrified. That was what the Philadelphia Center perfected: the work of making a life navigable again.

The Philadelphia Center's story, in the end, is an accumulation of increments—a record of scenes that make a city livable. Today the Center provides Ryan White Part B direct services to more than 750 clients and their families. Its programs include prevention and outreach—mobile testing, condom distribution, PrEP navigation, a needle exchange program, STD testing, and community education—as well as support groups and case management that meet the evolving needs of those living long-term with HIV. The work is bigger now, but still built from the same units it started with one call returned, one form completed, one person kept in care.

The organization is no longer funded to operate a separate advocacy department or residential recovery program, but it continues to steward Mercy Center, now serving an aging population and others in need of supportive housing. What began as an emergency refuge and hospice matured into long-term stability. From that small first grant and a handful of volunteers grew a durable network of care, less glamorous than protest but no less radical: the daily insistence that people deserve to survive.

The same hands that once held protest signs now pass medication across clinic counters, plan health fairs, and steady those newly diagnosed through the first nights of disbelief. Its hallways echo less with crisis and more with continuity—the hum of computers, laughter from a support group down the hall, the rhythm of daily life. Each piece of it—every counseling session, every test, every delivered meal—is another quiet defiance against the years when the city chose distance.

It would be wrong to say the Philadelphia Center ended the stigma associated with HIV and AIDS. It did not end death either. But it would be truer to say it changed the terms. When people say Shreveport did not retreat, they mean enough of its people learned, through ACT UP Shreveport and the Philadelphia Center, how to lean in. They mean a clinic became a network; a grant became groceries, counseling, and rides to appointments; a nurse's witness became a movement's spine; a mother's chair in a circle of grieving women became permission for others to stay; and loved ones' names stitched into a quilt became reason enough for a city to open its wallet, its heart, and its mouth.

By the time new drug therapies lengthened lives into decades, the Philadelphia Center had already taught Shreveport how to hold both grief and longevity. It adapted to adherence counseling, the economics of long-term care, and the burdens of survival—loneliness, depression, the discipline of daily pills, the bruise of returning to work in offices that still made jokes. It trained clients to be their own advocates and institutions to listen. The years no longer galloped; they gathered. And in that gathering, the Center's work became less about emergency and more about endurance—the work of keeping people here.

You can hear that work in what people remember. Ask the staff and they'll tell you about the filing cabinet that jammed every Thursday, the copier that rattled, the day the phones went quiet for an hour and everyone froze because they had learned to measure the world by rings. Ask the clients and they'll tell you about a particular chair in a particular room where someone spoke their name with respect. Ask Shreveport and it will point to a building, a bridge, and a candlelight vigil and say, not proudly but with a certain plainness: We learned. We learned because of ACT UP Shreveport and the Philadelphia Center—because they would not let us forget.

Years later, that ritual widened. On December 1, 2015, the city formally marked World AIDS Day at the Robinson Film Center in downtown Shreveport with a mayoral proclamation, a keynote speech by Robert Darrow, and a screening of early footage from *Small Town Rage*—the story Shreveport had finally learned to tell about itself. The sound of names carried through the night, and for once, Shreveport did not look away.

Today, the Philadelphia Center employs thirty-four staff members—case managers, clinicians, educators, and advocates—each carrying forward the same mission that began in grief and defiance. What started as a handful of volunteers and activists has become a lasting institution of care, proof that compassion, once organized, can outlast crisis. The scale is new; the intention remains the same.

By then, the Center had become what Shreveport once said it could never sustain—a permanence built from persistence, shaped by the LGBTQ+ community that carried it forward. The Philadelphia Center did not arrive with a ribbon-cutting or ceremony. It arrived with a key in a lock and a phone that wouldn't stop. It stayed long enough to turn emergency into structure. Its legacy can't be summed up in programs or proclamations. It's found in something smaller and truer: a room with fluorescent lights, a desk stacked with forms, and a counselor asking, "What do you need today?" and meaning it. That habit of meeting fear with order and shame with welcome remade a corner of the South. From those rooms, the narrative extends outward to memory, witness, and the record that refused to disappear. In those rooms, the ordinary became testimony, written not on film but in the lives it sustained.

And yet, institutions alone do not preserve history. Buildings hold services; people hold stories. The Philadelphia Center kept bodies alive, but memory required another kind of insistence. The names spoken at vigils, the quilt panels lifted skyward—all of it risked softening into nostalgia unless someone chose to record and preserve it while the witnesses were still alive.

What the Center preserved was not only life but continuity. People who might have disappeared remained visible—to themselves, to each other, to a city still learning how to see. That visibility accumulated over time, building a record that existed even before it was written down.

Care had stabilized the present. The next task was to preserve the past—not through policy or structure, but through story, through film, through the deliberate act of remembering in the making of *Small Town Rage*.

CHAPTER 9
THE MAKING OF *SMALL TOWN RAGE*

"We had to get it on camera, or it was going to be lost forever."
—Raydra Hall, codirector of
Small Town Rage: Fighting Back in the Deep South

What follows is my story—how Raydra Hall and I came to document ACT UP Shreveport and preserve the record of a movement that refused to disappear.

The silences of Shreveport had always been dangerous. In the early years of AIDS, it cut people off from care, split families, and shortened lives that might have lasted longer if anyone had spoken. By the second decade of the new millennium, a different silence had begun to gather— not the virus itself, but the memory of the fight against it. The names, the marches, the fury of ACT UP Shreveport could vanish again unless we caught them on film.

The idea for the film did not arrive with fanfare. It began in the spring of 2012, in a classroom at Bossier Parish Community College, where Raydra and I were enrolled in Filmmaking 101. Instructor Rusty Johnson urged students to think beyond paper assignments. The room itself was ordinary—fluorescent lights, mismatched desks, the low hum of a projector warming up—but what was being suggested inside it was not. For most students, it was an assignment. For us, it was beginning to feel like something else entirely. He introduced us to documentary forms—vérité-style handheld work, formal interviews, narrated arcs, experimental essays—and explained that most projects begin with an outline and build toward the lens. This time, the process would turn inside out. After one class, I returned home and shared my plan with my roommate Deborah Allen: a documentary on the role of organized religion in Louisiana politics. Deborah listened, then said, "Why not make it about ACT UP Shreveport instead?" That conversation reframed the entire project.

The students were an unlikely mix—Kirk Fontenot, Benn Ryan, Raydra Hall, and me. At first, the project was just coursework. But when the subject turned to AIDS in Shreveport, something shifted. The assignment stopped being about grades and became about memory and survival. We made an unusual choice: no outline, no script. Each conversation would stand on its own, and only later would the structure emerge. What began as an academic exercise was becoming an act of preservation.

The team soon shifted. Benn Ryan drifted away to other priorities. Kirk Fontenot, who had worked with Raydra and me at the Deaf Action Center, eventually moved on as well. With him went some of the early ease of collaboration. What began as four voices narrowed to two. The change was gradual, then complete. Conversations that once filled a room now settled into quieter exchanges—fewer perspectives, but sharper focus. What remained was not easier, only clearer. From then on, Raydra and I carried the work forward.

Our partnership was both unlikely and necessary. I carried what Raydra later described as the insider's urgency—the perspective of someone who had lived inside the story, who knew the people not as subjects but as friends and neighbors in a city that often denied their existence. I carried the memory of funerals, of names already sewn into the quilt.

Raydra, coming from outside Shreveport, brought distance that became clarity. She had not lived the same losses, but she could see what years of silence had blurred. My instinct was to preserve; hers was to pare down, shaping a story that could reach audiences beyond northwest Louisiana. Together, we made the film.

We rarely argued. When differences arose, we leaned into conversation until consensus took shape. I pressed for depth, unwilling to lose nuance; Raydra pressed for clarity, shaping the story so it could travel. The rhythm of our work was dialogue, not conflict—a steady back-and-forth that brought balance. Carrying the film from a classroom idea to international screenings deepened the partnership.

Making the film required both excavation and confrontation. Survivors were scattered across states and across lives. Some had fled Louisiana altogether; others withdrew into privacy, wary of reopening wounds. Tracking them down was detective work. Convincing them to speak was harder. Silence had become muscle memory—the survival instinct of a place that punished truth. Breaking it required trust, patience, and sometimes the courage to say aloud what had been locked away for decades.

The interviews were never neutral. The camera was invitation and threat in equal measure. For some, it became a confessional—a chance to speak what had been sealed for decades. For others, it was unbearable, a reminder of wounds that refused to close. Raydra later said she could feel the heaviness before a word was spoken—the silence that seemed to sit in the chair beside her.

Most interviews took place in the homes of the film's primary subjects. That choice mattered. At kitchen tables and in living rooms, the exchanges became intimate. It felt less like journalism than invitation— as filmmakers, but also as witnesses entrusted with truths long withheld. Each room carried its own layer of story: the pictures on the walls, the light across worn furniture, the pauses in breath, the spaces where silence had lived. Sometimes the camera caught what words could not: a hand tightening around the edge of a chair, a glance toward a photograph just out of frame, the way someone inhaled before saying a name they had not spoken aloud in years. One of those interviews—Gary Cathey's— was filmed inside George's Grill, the diner where this story first found its voice.

And then the silence broke. James Smith, speaking of the months he sat beside Chuck Selber's bed as his body failed, dissolved into tears that blurred the lens. What shattered him was not only Chuck's dying but also the memory of Kurt Pickett, once his lover. The weight of both—one friend, one love—forced him to pause before he could continue. Deborah Allen, fierce and steady in so much of her life, turned away from the camera when memory pressed too hard. Even Robert Darrow's parents, Bill and Jean, who had carried stigma beside their son for decades, found themselves naming truths they had once locked away. Jean said, "It wasn't that he had AIDS. It was that we might lose him."

Nearly every interview, in one way or another, ended in tears. Jean Darrow wiped her eyes and managed a small, trembling smile. "I knew this was going to be hard," she said. "I had no idea it would come back so fast—and hurt this much."

The toll fell on us too. After interviews, Raydra and I often sat wordless, unable to process what we had just heard. We were not parachuting journalists collecting sound bites. We were witnesses to the most painful moments in the lives of people we loved. There was no clean separation between the work and the rest of our lives. The stories followed us into silence—into car rides, into kitchens, into nights where sleep came late or not at all. Every confession became something we carried home with us. 'We brought those stories home every time," I said later.

As the interviews accumulated, the urgency moved beyond living rooms and into public space. The film's Kickstarter campaign carried it outward. Running from August to October 2015, it declared: "If these stories are not preserved, they will vanish. This film is not only about history but about dignity, about refusing to let silence win again." The campaign drew support from Broadway Cares / Equity Fights AIDS, the Jewish Federation, the Philadelphia Center, and dozens of individuals. Messages came in from people we had never met—some with stories of their own, others simply saying thank you for remembering what they feared would be forgotten. The film was already beginning to travel before it was finished.

During the filming of the Kickstarter video, emotion overtook me. As I spoke about what Raydra and I had already captured—especially the interview with Bill and Jean Darrow, Robert's parents—my voice broke. Later, those who watched the raw footage said that moment became the heartbeat of the campaign. It was not a performance.

One meeting in New York changed everything. During a trip for my Central Park wedding to Troy in May 2015, Robert Darrow and I met with Tom Viola, executive director of Broadway Cares/Equity Fights AIDS, hoping the organization might come aboard as an executive producer. The conversation began slowly. We made our case, asked for support, and the room fell quiet. Then Robert mentioned, almost as an

　　　　　　　　DR. DAVID W. HYLAN

afterthought, that we had a trailer. Tom agreed to watch. He pulled it up on his computer. The room went silent. When the screen went dark, he turned toward us, eyes wet. "You have your money," he said. "Everything you asked for."

The campaign raised nearly five times its goal. Every dollar went directly to the film—production, editing, promotion, and festival screenings. Neither Raydra nor I received any of it; it all went into the work.

Gregory Kallenberg had already been reshaping the city's creative landscape—not just as a promoter, but as a creator who understood the work from the inside out. What began as the Louisiana Film Prize, now simply Film Prize, grew into the Prize Foundation, an umbrella for Prize Fest and its expanding slate of competitions—Film Prize, Food Prize, Comedy Prize, Music Prize, Taco Wars—each designed to sharpen craft, foster collaboration, and create real opportunity for artists. It wasn't just about showcasing talent; it was about building a sustainable creative economy. At the same time, Gregory launched *The Rational Middle*, an award-winning collaborative focused on bringing clarity to complex, often divisive issues through documentary, writing, podcasts, and digital media—work grounded in facts, context, and the belief that meaningful conversation is still possible.

Another key moment came during a lunch with Gregory, a close friend, who cut straight to the heart of it. "Who will edit the film for you?" he asked. When I told him Raydra and I planned to do it ourselves, he didn't hesitate. After all the filming and the intimacy of hearing those stories firsthand, objectivity would be nearly impossible. "If you try," he said, "your film will likely be four and a half hours long." We listened.

We had already worked with Clint McCommon and John Chambers, videographers who had collaborated with us on Deaf Action Center projects. We trusted their craft and their collaboration. With funding secured and a clearer sense of what the film required, we brought Clint McCommon and John Chambers on to the project—a decision that saved it.

As funding secured the film's survival, the circle of collaborators widened. Clint and John expanded the team, each addition widening the film's reach beyond the edit room. Photographer Mollie Corbit captured headshots of Raydra and me and helped coordinate the Kickstarter video that carried our plea to supporters. Anton Winder later developed an interactive touchscreen program allowing viewers to explore raw footage by theme and topic. Donated to the Philadelphia Center, the unit became an educational tool and a living extension of the documentary.

Our first meeting with the Fairfield team wasn't in an edit room but on the balcony of the Robinson Film Center's Abby Singer Bistro, overlooking Texas Street. Around the table sat John Chambers, Clint McCommon, Raydra Hall, Anton Winder, Mollie Corbit, and me. Clint remembered it clearly: "David and Raydra came in with this urgency. It wasn't just another project for them—you could feel it was personal. John and I knew right away that whatever we did had to honor that."

Once that first meeting gave way to work, the limits set in. Hours of footage could not fit into the film. Raydra later said, "There were whole stories we could not include—important material left behind simply because time would not allow."

By then, the story was holding—but it still needed a voice to guide it forward.

The first time I tried to bring Lance Bass—the *NSYNC* star—to Shreveport, it didn't happen.

I was organizing guests for the North Louisiana Gay Film Festival and reached out through his representatives. They checked with him. He was interested. Then the calendar closed in—conflicts, commitments, and scheduling that couldn't be worked out. It fell through.

But he had said yes, or something close to it. That stayed with me.

Later, when Raydra and I began looking for a narrator, we started where everyone starts—with names that already carry weight. Morgan Freeman. Alan Cumming. James Earl Jones. We reached out—or tried to. But the voices felt too familiar, too recognizable. They would bring presence, but not connection.

Raydra was the one who circled back.

"What about Lance?" she said.

She remembered how excited I'd been the first time. And this time, it made more sense. He was from Ellisville, Mississippi—just a few hours from Shreveport. Southern. Gay. Close enough to the story to understand its shape.

I called his agency again.

The same woman answered. She remembered me. She remembered the festival, the conflict, the near miss. I told her about the film—what we were trying to do, why it mattered. I could hear it shift in her voice,

     DR. DAVID W. HYLAN

that moment when a conversation stops being polite and starts becoming real.

I was in the office when the call came in. She called back the next day. "He's a yes," she said. "He's really excited about it."

For a moment, everything else just... stopped. I felt a rush of relief and something close to elation—not just that he had said yes, but because I knew what his voice would mean for the film. We had found it.

Then the work began.

We needed a studio in Los Angeles. An engineer. A schedule that could hold. Following a friend of Raydra's recommendation, we found The Nook Studio, with Ethan Walter and Sean Williamson, and began refining the narration—cutting it down, shaping it so the voice would carry only what the interviews could not. The story had to belong to the people who lived it. The narrator would only guide it forward.

The Kickstarter funds got us to Los Angeles. Raydra, Clint, and I flew in the day before the session and planned to arrive early.

We didn't. The address led us to the wrong building—an industrial stretch with a sign that simply read "studio." No movement. No sound. Just the wrong place. I called Ethan.

"That's the old address," he said. "We moved."

The new location was near our hotel. Close enough to be easy. It wasn't.

We hit the 405, and traffic didn't crawl—it stopped. Completely. The three of us sat there watching the clock—ten minutes to the session, then past it, then thirty minutes past—calling, updating, apologizing, inching forward because there was nothing else we could do.

By the time we pulled into the parking lot, we were nearly fifty minutes late. I called again. "We're here. We're walking in."

Lance was already inside, sitting with Ethan and Sean—calm, patient, waiting.

We walked in carrying all that tension with us, and Lance just... took it out of the room. Smiled. Told us it was fine. That this was Los Angeles. This happens.

He had the script in his hand—marked, prepared.

When he stepped behind the glass, it was immediate. He didn't simply read the words. He worked them. Between takes, he would pause, look through the glass, and ask if it felt right. Not just correct, but true. And when a line seemed not to land—when even we could feel something on the page wasn't yet settling into place—Lance offered suggestions. He never assumed the role of editor, never inserted himself as if the script were his to shape. What he offered came from somewhere else: a shared concern that the story be told the right way. It was an indication that he had bought into the project, that he was no longer an outsider looking in but part of something taking shape in real time. He wanted it to be as right as we did. He was not performing the words so much as stepping into the story.

We had booked two hours. Even starting late, we finished in less than one.

Afterward, we took photos—one with him turned away, one facing forward. We posted the first with a simple line:

"Guess who is narrating *Small Town Rage*."

A week later, we posted the second.

"Lance Bass."

The narration was never meant to lead the story—only to connect where the interviews could not.

Clint admitted the scale of the project was daunting. Taking on something this size scared him. He didn't want to screw it up, but he also didn't want to say no. Pulling it off, he said, left him proud—not because it was flawless, but because he had promised and delivered. John described it as a turning point for their work together. They had produced documentaries before, but never one that mattered like this. "For once, we weren't just creating content," John later said. "We were making something that carried weight."

At the Fairfield studio, the walls stacked with tapes and hard drives became the work in front of us. Every cut carried consequence. The timeline on the screen became a kind of ledger—what stayed, what disappeared, what had to be trusted to memory instead of film. I wanted to keep everything; Raydra pressed for what would carry through; Clint and John worked to shape coherence without losing the story. "Each minute cut away felt like a piece of someone's life," I later recalled.

Not everyone wanted the past reopened. Some families refused interviews, fearful of what might be unearthed. Others worried how their loved ones would be portrayed. Institutions that had once turned their backs on AIDS patients offered little help—not from malice, but from shame. Hospitals, churches, and political offices struggled to defend their history of neglect and stigma. Archives were thin, records scarce.

We pieced together fragments, reconstructing what others might have preferred to leave in darkness.

Even within ACT UP's surviving circle, tensions resurfaced—disputes about outing Congressman Jim McCrery, how confrontational to be, whether rage had gone too far. That unease carried into the edit room. Keeping McCrery in the film risked blowback; leaving him out felt like erasing truth. We chose to keep it. "The film had to let people speak in their own voices, even when those voices clashed," Raydra later said.

Those tensions followed us into the edit room. Each interview was precious; each story demanded space. The hardest work was deciding what to let go. "It felt like disloyalty at times," Raydra later said, "but the question never changed: what will carry through?"

For Clint, the answer came in structure. He thought of the film in chapters, each with its own arc: sadness, anger, and even a few moments of levity. The biggest turns were saved for the end. Rhythm mattered. It was the only way to keep an audience from being crushed under the weight all at once. "What will hold a stranger's attention long enough to hear?" Clint asked himself in the edit room. Raydra and I, ever the archivists, wanted to preserve everything, fearing omission meant silence winning again. But film demanded sacrifice. The result was compromise—painful but necessary.

The premiere carried its own tensions. Families who had once shunned conversations about AIDS now sat in the theater, watching images of their sons, brothers, and friends. Some entered reluctantly; others stayed away altogether. Their absence was felt.

The Robinson Film Center hosted three sold-out screenings in its largest 130-seat theater. Every chair was filled, with extra seats brought in. The air in the room felt dense, as if the audience understood before the first frame that what they were about to watch belonged to them. Some audience members stood in the back or lined the side walls. Behind the scenes, tensions surfaced between the filmmakers and the festival's coordinating committee—it was the first time the festival had hosted a premiere, and expectations sometimes collided.

During the credits, the top inch and a half of local obituaries scrolled across the screen—names of people from north Louisiana who had died of AIDS. Clint and John paired the sequence with a quiet, elegiac score centered on those who did not survive.

Clint later described sitting in the back of the Robinson Film

Center that night. "When the obituaries rolled, I realized I knew some of them—classmates' families, people from my neighborhood. It stopped being history at a distance; it became personal. I thought, this is Shreveport's story too, not just ACT UP's. That scroll broke me." The names did not move quickly. They lingered just long enough to be read, to be recognized—or to be realized as someone no one had spoken about in years.

Raydra and I pushed back against festival organizers who suggested stopping the film once the credits began to make time for a Q&A. "We told them—don't you dare," we said, insisting the credits roll in full. Clint agreed, recalling, "Those names weren't just credits; they were part of the story. For many, it was the only time their names had ever been honored on a screen."

Gary Cathey described the moment: "It was humbling to watch the premiere audience live our journey with us. They showed up. They listened. They learned. What struck me most was their graciousness—staying after the credits, talking, asking questions."

Deborah Allen said, "You could feel the weight of history in the room—people laughed, cried, and sat in silence long after the credits rolled." Robert Darrow added, "The premiere was overwhelming. In that theater, you could feel the tears, the gasps, the applause that refused to end."

One of the deepest honors of the premiere was the presence of Chuck Selber's family—his mother Flo, his brother, his sister, nieces, and nephews—all gathered to witness his story on screen. For Raydra and me, embracing those who had loved Chuck most mattered. Bonds formed that night have endured.

As the lights rose, people clutched friends, partners, and family. Some embraced; others reached for hands they had not held in years. The film forced open memories, but it also allowed space for acknowledgment. For many, it was the first time they could speak openly about loss.

What unfolded in that theater did not remain confined to applause or tears. For many in the audience, the film was as much mirror as memory. It brought into view Shreveport's difficult truths—churches, religion, and hypocrisy. For some, it was a reckoning.

Even the local press had begun, decades earlier, to shift. *The Shreveport Times* urged readers to find compassion for gays and lesbians, and in another editorial insisted it took courage simply to live honestly. Those voices foreshadowed what the film would later bring into focus.

The reception extended beyond Shreveport and across Louisiana, and in 2018 the Louisiana Endowment for the Humanities named *Small Town Rage* Film of the Year. Other awards followed. But the most telling moments were quieter—viewers leaving theaters in tears, whispering for the first time, "I didn't know."

At Philadelphia QFest, the film received the Gittings International Human Rights Award—named for activist Barbara Gittings, whose work advanced LGBTQ+ visibility and equality. The team later laughed about the trophy's distinctive shape, affectionately nicknaming it "the Vagina Award." It became its own story—a reminder that even in grief, humor had its place, just as Chuck Selber had taught.

Festivals followed in New Orleans, Toronto, Amsterdam, at Cinema on the Bayou, in Glasgow, and at the North Louisiana Gay and Lesbian Film Festival in Shreveport—today known as the OUTnorthLa Film Festival. At each screening, in every festival, and in every country where it was shown, the film received awards—its reception as consistent as it was unexpected.

Beyond the awards and festival applause, the film became something quieter and more personal. For some survivors, it offered release. Speaking on camera—or watching their younger selves reflected back—unclenched something that had been held for decades. It did not erase grief, but it eased it.

The film did not affect only those on camera. It changed the people behind it as well. Clint later said, "I was just a carefree high school kid when people here were fighting for their lives. Working on this humbled me. It made me respect activism in a way I never had. I've marched in protests since then—Black Lives Matter, women's rights—because I finally understood how hard it is to stand up. The people in this film made me want to do better."

Reliving the process—filming, editing, music, the final cut—was painful. But there was pride in what emerged. What began in a college classroom had become something that lasted.

Even as festivals and awards affirmed the film's impact, it was never enough. The film had done what it could. It had opened the door, held it, and asked people to step through it. But there was more behind it—stories still waiting, voices not yet heard. Ninety-eight minutes could hold only part of what had been lived. Stories were left out. That incompleteness led me to the book—not to repeat the film, but to extend it, to give space to what could not fit within a frame. As Raydra said, the film kept silence from swallowing ACT UP Shreveport completely. What endured was what followed—how those who lived it carried that history forward into their own lives, shaping what remained into legacy and aftermath.

CHAPTER 10
LEGACY AND AFTERMATH

"We may not have changed everything overnight, but we made silence, judgment, and hypocrisy impossible to ignore. We dragged them into the open, cracked their hold, and demanded dignity instead."
—Deborah Allen, ACT UP Shreveport member

"We were the smallest city in the country with an ACT UP chapter," Gary Cathey would later recall. In Shreveport, that meant defiance unfolded in full view—under the weight of faith, power, and a community that often chose judgment over care. Churches preached mercy while condemning the sick. Officials urged patience while people died. Families turned away from their own. The cost of speaking was never abstract—it was personal, visible, and immediate. It showed up in small ways first—a phone call not returned, a shift cut from the schedule, a look that lingered too long in the grocery store. Then it widened. Doors closed. Invitations stopped. Silence took on weight.

The activists who carried that defiance did so not in anonymity but in full view of neighbors who knew their names, families, and jobs. No other city, Gary said, faced the same level of hostility from its own community. Every protest, every headline, every act of care carried risk—backlash, exile, being marked. And still they chose to speak.

Hospitals turned patients away. Families whispered but refused to name the truth. In churches, pulpits thundered judgment louder than mercy. The same voices that claimed the gospel ignored its simplest command: "I was hungry, and you gave me food... I was a stranger, and you welcomed me." Yet not all faith hardened into condemnation. Some learned to separate belief from cruelty, carrying forward a quieter conviction rooted in mercy. Justin Normand would later describe that shift not as rejection, but as reclamation—faith stripped of power and spectacle, still capable of demanding compassion.

In that absence, ACT UP Shreveport became a mirror—showing the city what compassion looked like when institutions failed. Robert Darrow called it "the chemistry of a group of very talented, competent people with honor," a gathering that turned outrage into organization. They built what did not exist: testing, housing, counseling, and eventually the Philadelphia Center. What began as protest became infrastructure.

What endured was not just protest, but what it made possible. The creation of the Philadelphia Center marked a turning point—those voices became the backbone of care in Northwest Louisiana. It outlived the anger, the fear, and even many who built it. The Center did not erase the city's cruelty, but it ensured something remained in its wake.

ACT UP Shreveport rose small in number and far from national networks, but unafraid to name cruelty and expose injustice. Deborah Allen later described their defiance as uniquely Southern—rooted in faith, family, and a stubborn belief that dignity belonged to everyone.

Every action carried consequences. In New York or San Francisco, a protest might mean a headline. In Shreveport, it meant your boss seeing you on the evening news, your pastor turning you into a sermon, your family severing ties. Gary remembered that risk clearly—the knowledge that speaking out could cost your job, your home, even your safety. The danger deepened their resolve. In a city where silence was expected, visibility itself became defiance. To be seen meant being remembered—and being remembered meant there was no way back to anonymity. Once a name appeared in print or on a protest sign, it stayed.

The price of visibility was enormous. It was also the only weapon they had. To be seen was to exist—to refuse the lie that AIDS could remain hidden. Kenny King called it courage born of necessity—an insistence that people with AIDS would not vanish quietly.

Years later, Kenny said that showing up at all—placing his name alongside the words AIDS and ACT UP—was a conscious act of defiance. His press releases and poster designs claimed space in a city that preferred erasure. Each flyer, each design, each headline became a record that refused to fade. The art was never decoration; it was documentation. The ink, the layout, the placement of a headline—each choice fixed a moment in time. What might have been dismissed as a flyer became evidence.

Their first achievement was survival—of bodies, of community, of the idea that resistance could exist here at all. Jason Bratlie, who joined briefly on a trip to Atlanta, remembered being struck by that fact: ACT UP had taken root in Shreveport, of all places. This was a conservative town where raising awareness guaranteed ridicule. Yet there they were— visible, uncompromising, refusing to disappear.

But existence was never enough. Urgency drove them further. Robert Darrow remembered the fight to make clinical trials more inclusive, pressing for the participation of women, children, and people of color. Through their protests and actions, they became part of a national voice that helped shorten the drug-approval process. That shift was not abstract. It meant months gained where there had once been none—time to try a new regimen, time to sit at a table, time to be present in a life that had nearly been cut short. Alana Oldham pointed to their connection with the Americans with Disabilities Act, which ensured protections for people living with HIV and AIDS. Their impact reached beyond Shreveport, threading local courage into national reform.

Beneath the protests, ACT UP Shreveport was building—work that stretched from the hospital corridors of LSU Medical Center to the policy tables of Baton Rouge and, through ACT UP's national movement, to Capitol Hill. In the early 1990s, their pressure on local physicians and state officials echoed demands being made at the FDA and NIH: speed the trials, expand access, center the patient. They pushed for broader clinical trials, helping cut years from the approval of life-saving drugs. They demanded access to experimental treatments, forcing local hospitals into compassionate-use programs and national studies. At LSU Medical Center, where patients had been left unfed and unattended, they confronted neglect directly and modeled patient-centered care— humane, immediate, inclusive.

Their influence did not stop at medicine. By naming homophobia as a public-health threat, they reframed how care was understood in the

South. Their activism intersected with the broader LGBTQ+ rights movement, linking the fight for people with AIDS to dignity and equality. They joined national efforts pressing for insurance reform and the inclusion of women in benefits and trials. In Louisiana, Viral Disease Clinics and expanded HIV funding bore the mark of that work.

In the Deep South, where stigma still shaped care, their influence turned tangible. Their enduring achievement was the Philadelphia Center—born from ACT UP Shreveport's demand for care, an institution that outlived the protests and carried the work into services, case management, prevention, and advocacy. Deborah remembered how disorienting that transition was—moving from confrontation into negotiation—but she knew it was necessary. "The fight for dignity couldn't stay only in the streets," she said. "It had to be written into policies, programs, and institutions."

For Kenny, its creation closed a circle—the energy once poured into confrontation now building the structures protest had demanded. Bryan Sullivan recalled how it was built from within—the same people who carried placards became the managers, directors, and staff providing food, housing, and care. Alana Oldham called it "critical," not only for services but for insisting that people in the region deserved dignity. Robert saw ACT UP Shreveport and the Center as inseparable, one born from the other. While similar centers across the country collapsed or merged, the Philadelphia Center endured. It remains a reminder that a small group of activists in Shreveport forced a city—and a state—to face what it would rather have ignored.

During the protests, the effort was already shifting. Robert started the Baja Beach Club to raise money for the Philadelphia Center before it even had an office, later bringing Kenny on board to run it. He turned nightlife into philanthropy, channeling profits directly into building what ACT UP Shreveport had demanded.

Recognition came later. In the eighties and early nineties, the city felt fixed in its judgment. But the ground did shift. Editorial boards that once turned away began to call for compassion. Robert saw it when ACT UP Shreveport members were finally allowed to testify before the Louisiana Department of Health and Hospitals—voices entering rooms that had once barred them. Between 1992 and 1995, the tone began to change. The state could no longer pretend it was someone else's problem.

That institutional shift soon took on a public face. Newspapers ran editorials urging readers to "find humanity for gays and lesbians," reframing suffering not as sin but as a summons to mercy. Faith leaders and physicians who had once stood silent began lending their names to World AIDS Day programs. Entertainment columns promoted cabaret benefits for the Philadelphia Center—hotel ballrooms and neighborhood clubs where drag performers, jazz musicians, and clergy shared the same stage. The Florentine Club, once a private supper club, opened its doors for benefit nights that blended laughter and loss. The crowds changed too. Faces that had once turned away were now familiar. Some came quietly, standing at the edges of rooms before stepping further in. Others arrived openly, no longer pretending distance. People who had once crossed the street now bought tickets and came inside.

By the late 1990s, civic leaders issued proclamations for World AIDS Day. Schools hosted quilt displays. Cabaret benefits for the Philadelphia Center drew the city into evenings where grief and celebration met. What had once been whispered was now spoken publicly—through microphones, through programs, through presence. The city's tone had changed—not completely, not evenly—but enough that compassion no longer required apology. Year after year, the Auction Against AIDS became a gathering that sustained the work, where art and memory met to carry it forward.

For Richard Kightlinger, change was intimate. What happened in the streets carried into kitchens and living rooms. The protests gave him language, gave him strength, and gave him a community that could not be erased. He later said ACT UP Shreveport strengthened his decision to come out to his family—an act of honesty that carried its own risk. There was no guarantee of acceptance waiting on the other side. Only the certainty that silence was no longer possible. ACT UP Shreveport was the first chapter in Louisiana, preceding even New Orleans in the early years of the crisis. His courage was part of that first spark of visibility in the state.

Before ACT UP Shreveport, even acknowledging a gay population in Shreveport was unthinkable, Bryan remembered. ACT UP forced the city to admit what it had denied—that gay people lived here, that they were visible, that they were dying. Once admitted, the conversation could not return to what it had been. At LSU Medical Center, protocols shifted—not out of gratitude, but because activists left no choice. "When you know better, you do better," Bryan said—and ACT UP had forced the knowledge.

The work did not end. Each carried it forward differently. Robert Darrow made it a lifelong practice of speaking truth to power. Dave Herrell learned to channel outrage without letting it consume him. Richard Kightlinger turned activism into art, where creativity became resistance. Bryan Sullivan described himself not as loud, but as proud. Cecil Thad Coburn, less confrontational by nature, gave his time steadily, quiet constancy as its own form of resistance. For Alana Oldham the experience reshaped her sense of what was possible, giving her the courage to stand on her own and build a life far beyond Shreveport, living for decades outside the United States. Justin Normand came to see activism as obligation. "To whom much is given, much shall be required," he said, not as warning, but as mandate. Jason Bratlie carried it into the classroom, shaping future activists. Deborah Allen sustained the work through decades of advocacy, moving from protest into institutions determined to change them from within.

Judy Williams carried it forward in another way—the work reshaping her into someone who understood speaking up as responsibility rather than choice. "It raised my consciousness," she said, "about the responsibility to speak up when something is wrong." What remained was not a single act, but a shift in who she was: the quiet understanding that silence was never neutral, and that dignity required a voice.

Time carried them forward in different directions, but never far from what they had built together. For many, survival meant remaking family when the one they were born into fell away. Justin was not alone in that loss—he had lost much of his family of origin to bigotry decades ago, a fracture that never healed, only redefined belonging. In its place, he built a smaller circle, a chosen family forged through shared conviction rather than blood. It was the same instinct that had shaped ACT UP Shreveport in crisis: creating community where institutions had failed.

For Gary Cathey, that inheritance became a source of healing. ACT UP forged friendships into lifelong family and gave him an outlet for his need to act. Years later, the documentary *Small Town Rage* reopened that history in a way that helped him believe in his worth. Being asked to speak at screenings—from PACE to Louisiana Tech to the Louisiana School for Math, Science, and the Arts—became acts of renewal. For all of them, what had once been loss began, in small ways, to return as recognition. Not complete, not repaired—but acknowledged.

Even warriors fall, and many did. Their names are not all recorded here, but their absence is felt. Those who survived carry them forward—in stories, in photographs, in fragments of memory that refuse to settle. In the telling, some found those memories rising again, sharp and immediate, as if no time had passed. The weight remains—and so does what they changed.

What they built did not erase what was lost. It made it visible. It gave it shape. And it ensured it would be carried forward—not as absence alone, but as presence.

ACKNOWLEDGMENTS

This book was born from the courage of people who refused to disappear quietly. It would not exist without the men and women of ACT UP Shreveport—those who lived the story, those who told it, and those whose voices I now carry only in memory. To everyone who opened a door, shared a story, or trusted me with their grief, their fury, their laughter, or their truth—thank you. Your lives shaped these pages.

My deepest gratitude goes to Dr. Robert Darrow, whose editorial guidance, historical insight, and steadfast friendship guided this project from its earliest moments. His fingerprints are on every chapter. Robert has been a partner in memory, a mirror for honesty, and the quiet constant I leaned on more times than I can count.

To the families and friends of Chuck Selber, Joe DeSantis, Kurt Pickett, and Chris Free; and to the many people who gave their time across one interview or many: Nancy Zeidman Accado, Deborah Allen, Sharon Adler, Bruce Allen, Jason Bratlie, Gary Cathey, Chad Chromer, Cecil Thad Coburn, Yeona DaCosta-Auld, Mical DeBrow, Jill Selber Handaly, Micah Harold, Ashley Hazzelton, Dave Herrell, Candace Higginbotham, David Holland, Victor Jackson, Kenny King, Richard Kightlinger, Mark Anthony Lindsey, DeDe DeSantis McClamroch, Clint McCommon, Tracy Murrell, Gerardo Nigron, Justin Normand, Alana Oldham, Kenneth Peoples, Flo Selber and her family, Phyllis Selber, Sara Speer Selber, James Smith, Marcus Spurlock, Sandy Selber

Sturm, Bryan Sullivan, Bob Tatum, Greg Tolman, Judy Williams, Buddy Williamson, Jay Zeidman, Mark Zeidman, Leslie Zeidman—thank you for trusting me with your voices, your memories, and your histories.

I owe special gratitude to Kay Zeidman, Chuck Selber's sister, whose generosity extended far beyond interview hours. She opened her family's archives, shared documents and photographs, and welcomed my many follow-up questions. Through her openness, she allowed me to see inside the Selber family's story with uncommon depth. That trust was an honor, and I carried it with care.

I am grateful to Bobby Fierseler for generously sharing his research on the history of Greater Louisiana AIDS Defense (GLAD). His documentation and willingness to provide context helped ensure accuracy and depth in recounting this chapter of Louisiana's AIDS activism.

To Chris Miciotto, Hershey Krippendorf, and the staff, volunteers, and founders of the Philadelphia Center—thank you for decades of service and for stewarding a community when no one else would. Your archives, memory, and institutional courage are woven into the backbone of this book.

To the teams at LSU Shreveport Archives, to John Andrew Prime, whose journalism helped recover essential parts of this story; and to Nancy Morris Cook, whose interview and writing—including Chuck Selber's obituary—and perspective as a mother who lost a son to AIDS deepened this work immeasurably—thank you. To the libraries and journalists whose reporting formed the historical record: your work preserved what this city sometimes tried to forget.

To Raydra Hall, my friend and my filmmaking partner on *Small Town Rage*, thank you for the years we spent gathering these stories, preserving these voices, and standing witness together. Though this book is my own, its foundation was built through the work we did together, your belief in the project, and your commitment to the people whose lives we sought to honor.

To Jay Blotcher, whose editorial eye and professional guidance helped prepare this manuscript for its next life—thank you for your clarity, your rigor, and your honesty. Your work strengthened its structure and sharpened its purpose.

My deepest thanks to Raymond Luczak, whose design work elevated these words and shaped the book into something far greater than I imagined. He has given the people represented here a presence of dignity and clarity. I am especially grateful for his patience as I found my way through this first major writing project.

To Mark S. King, whose foreword frames this narrative with the wisdom of lived experience and the precision of a journalist who survived the epidemic and never stopped telling its truths—thank you. Your voice situates this story within a larger movement and honors the people whose lives fill these pages.

To Adrienne Critcher, friend and confidant for decades—thank you for reading the earliest full draft and for offering both your insight and your words for the back cover. Your encouragement and thoughtful critique helped this project find its footing when it needed it most.

To my friends and chosen family who listened to drafts, carried the weight of this story alongside me, and reminded me why it mattered— thank you for your patience and your faith.

And finally, to Troy—my husband, my grounding place, my partner in everything. Thank you for the quiet encouragement, the steady joy, and the unconditional love that made space for this book to exist. Your presence is the page I return to every time.

This project began as a documentary, but it became a restoration—a record of lives too often overlooked, a testament to rage harnessed in the service of justice, and a promise that silence will not have the last word.

SOURCE NOTES

INTRODUCTION

1. *Small Town Rage*—Documentary film (2016). Visual and narrative record confirming events, participant accounts, and protest actions of ACT UP Shreveport.

2. *Small Town Rage*—Final transcript (2012–2016). Primary oral-history backbone for verified quotations, speaker identification, and event reconstruction, including reflections by Deborah Allen, Gary Cathey, and other ACT UP members.

3. **ACT UP Shreveport—Organizational archive and protest documents (1989–1993).** Internal and public materials including memos, press releases, flyers, stickers, correspondence, and campaign messaging used to organize actions and communicate demands.

4. The *Advocate*—Publication (September 1992). Coverage of McCrery controversy and ACT UP response, highlighting public confrontation and media's role in shaping the crisis narrative.

5. The *Shreveport Times*—Newspaper (September 2, 1983; September 14, 1985; 1992; August 1993; December 1993). Coverage of AIDS cases, public response, funding disparities, and memorial reflections in Shreveport and surrounding areas.

6. Zinn Education Project—Publication (May 21, 1990). Overview of ACT UP's "Storm the NIH" action, framing the national movement and contextualizing regional responses like those in Shreveport.

7. **Deborah Allen**—Oral history interviews (*Small Town Rage* project,

2012–2017; Interviews, August 2025; November 2025; February 2026). Primary source for ACT UP formation, recruitment strategies, protest development, McCrery actions, and internal organizing in Shreveport.

8. **Gary Cathey—Oral history interviews (*Small Town Rage* project, 2012–2017; Interviews, September 2025; November 2025).** Source for ACT UP leadership, protest actions, and personal consequences of activism, particularly in Shreveport.

9. **ACT UP Oral History Project—Archival interviews and video materials (2001–present).** Participant testimony and documentation of national ACT UP actions, including the "Storm the NIH" demonstration and its implications for local movements like ACT UP Shreveport.

10. **Robert Darrow—Oral history interviews (*Small Town Rage* project, 2012-2017; Interviews, September 2025; October 2025).** Source for ACT UP formation, actions, strategy, medical advocacy, HIV treatments, and local response to AIDS in Shreveport, establishment of the Philadelphia Center.

CHAPTER 1: WELCOME TO SHREVEPORT

1. *Small Town Rage*—Documentary film (2016). Visual and narrative record confirming events, participant accounts, and protest actions of ACT UP Shreveport.

2. *Small Town Rage*—Final transcript (2012–2016). Primary oral-history backbone for verified quotations, speaker identification, and event reconstruction, including reflections by Deborah Allen, Gary Cathey, and other ACT UP members.

3. ACT UP Shreveport—Organizational archive and protest documents (1989–1993). Internal and public materials including memos, press releases, flyers, stickers, correspondence, and campaign messaging used to organize actions and communicate demands.

4. The *Shreveport Times*—Newspaper (September 2, 1983; September 14, 1985; 1992; August 1993; December 1993). Coverage of AIDS cases, public response, funding disparities, and memorial reflections in Shreveport and surrounding areas.

5. The *Advocate*—Publication (September 1992). Coverage of McCrery controversy and ACT UP response, highlighting public confrontation and media's role in shaping the crisis narrative.

6. Zinn Education Project—Publication (May 21, 1990). Overview of ACT UP's "Storm the NIH" action, framing the national movement and contextualizing regional responses like those in Shreveport.

7. Deborah Allen—Oral history interviews (*Small Town Rage* project, 2012–2017; Interviews, August 2025; November 2025; February 2026).

Primary source for ACT UP formation, recruitment strategies, protest development, McCrery actions, and internal organizing in Shreveport.

8. **Gary Cathey—Oral history interviews (*Small Town Rage* project, 2012–2017; Interviews, September 2025; November 2025).** Source for ACT UP leadership, protest actions, and personal consequences of activism, particularly in Shreveport.

9. **ACT UP Oral History Project—Archival interviews and video materials (2001–present).** Participant testimony and documentation of national ACT UP actions including the "Storm the NIH" demonstration and its implications for local movements like ACT UP Shreveport.

10. **Robert Darrow—Oral history interviews (*Small Town Rage* project, 2012–2017; Interviews, September 2025; October 2025).** Source for ACT UP formation, actions, strategy, medical advocacy, HIV treatments, and local response to AIDS in Shreveport, establishment of the Philadelphia Center.

11. **Gary Cathey—Correspondence (early 1990s).** Letter to Jim McCrery addressing AIDS policy positions, rhetoric, and constituent impact.

12. **The *Shreveport Journal*—Newspaper (June 12, 1985).** Coverage of ACT UP response to early AIDS cases and growing public awareness.

13. ***Bossier Press-Tribune*—Newspaper (July 1987).** Coverage of AIDS education efforts and regional awareness campaigns within Bossier City.

14. **Freeman and Harris Café—Organizational and community space (1980s–1990s).** Cultural hub for Black Shreveport, where political and social discussions intersected with activism, including early conversations around AIDS and community care.

15. **Louisiana Department of Health and Hospitals—State records (early 1990s).** Documentation of the state's response to the AIDS crisis and distribution of care, including funding discrepancies and regional health policies.

CHAPTER 2: DINNER AT GEORGE'S GRILL

1. ***Small Town Rage*—Documentary film (2016).** Visual and narrative record confirming events, participant accounts, and protest actions of ACT UP Shreveport.

2. ***Small Town Rage*—Final transcript (2012–2016).** Primary oral-history backbone for verified quotations, speaker identification, and event reconstruction, including reflections by Deborah Allen, Gary Cathey, and other ACT UP members.

3. **ACT UP Shreveport—Organizational archive and protest documents (1989–1993).** Internal and public materials including memos, press releases,

flyers, stickers, correspondence, and campaign messaging used to organize actions and communicate demands.

4. The *Advocate*—Publication (September 1992). Coverage of McCrery controversy and ACT UP response, highlighting public confrontation and media's role in shaping the crisis narrative.

5. The *Shreveport Times*—Newspaper (September 2, 1983; September 14, 1985; 1992; August 1993; December 1993). Coverage of AIDS cases, public response, funding disparities, and memorial reflections in Shreveport and surrounding areas.

6. Zinn Education Project—Publication (May 21, 1990). Overview of ACT UP's "Storm the NIH" action, framing the national movement and contextualizing regional responses like those in Shreveport.

7. Robert Darrow—Oral history interviews (*Small Town Rage* project, 2012–2017; Interviews, September 2025; October 2025). Source for ACT UP formation, actions, strategy, medical advocacy, HIV treatments, and local response to AIDS in Shreveport.

8. Deborah Allen—Oral history interviews (*Small Town Rage* project, 2012–2017; Interviews, August 2025; November 2025; February 2026). Primary source for ACT UP formation, recruitment strategies, protest development, McCrery actions, and internal organizing in Shreveport.

9. Gary Cathey—Oral history interviews (*Small Town Rage* project, 2012–2017; Interviews, September 2025; November 2025). Source for ACT UP leadership, protest actions, and personal consequences of activism, particularly in Shreveport.

10. ACT UP Oral History Project—Archival interviews and video materials (2001–present). Participant testimony and documentation of national ACT UP actions, including the "Storm the NIH" demonstration and its implications for local movements like ACT UP Shreveport.

11. Gary Cathey—Correspondence (early 1990s). Letter to Jim McCrery addressing AIDS policy positions, rhetoric, and constituent impact.

12. The *Shreveport Journal*—Newspaper (June 12, 1985). Coverage of ACT UP response to early AIDS cases and growing public awareness.

13. *Bossier Press-Tribune*—Newspaper (July 1987). Coverage of AIDS education efforts and regional awareness campaigns within Bossier City.

14. Freeman and Harris Café—Organizational and community space (1980s–1990s). Cultural hub for Black Shreveport, where political and social discussions intersected with activism, including early conversations around AIDS and community care.

15. Louisiana Department of Health and Hospitals—State records (early 1990s). Documentation of the state's response to the AIDS crisis and distribution of care, including funding discrepancies and regional health policies.

CHAPTER 3: CHUCK SELBER'S PURPOSEFUL ANGER

1. *Small Town Rage*—Documentary film (2016). Visual and narrative record confirming events, participant accounts, and protest actions of ACT UP Shreveport, including Chuck Selber's leadership and the group's local confrontations.
2. *Small Town Rage*—Final transcript (2012–2016). Primary oral-history backbone for verified quotations, speaker identification, and event reconstruction, particularly focusing on Chuck Selber, Gary Cathey, and other ACT UP members.
3. **ACT UP Shreveport—Organizational archive and protest documents (1989–1993).** Internal and public materials including memos, press releases, flyers, stickers, correspondence, and campaign messaging used to organize actions and communicate demands.
4. **The *Advocate*—Publication (September 1992).** Coverage of McCrery controversy and ACT UP response, highlighting public confrontation and media's role in shaping the crisis narrative.
5. **The *Shreveport Times*—Newspaper (September 2, 1983; September 14, 1985; 1992; August 1993; December 1993).** Coverage of AIDS cases, public response, funding disparities, and memorial reflections in Shreveport and surrounding areas.
6. **Zinn Education Project—Publication (May 21, 1990).** Overview of ACT UP's "Storm the NIH" action, framing the national movement and contextualizing regional responses like those in Shreveport.
7. **"Chuck Selber's Purposeful Anger"—article (December 2013).** Provides contextual framing of Selber's activism, including his use of anger as a tool for social change and supporting details about medical discrimination in Shreveport. Corroborates accounts of medical discrimination in Shreveport and contextualizes Selber's use of anger as an activist strategy.
8. **Deborah Allen—Oral history interviews (*Small Town Rage* project, 2012–2017; Interviews, August 2025; November 2025; February 2026).** Primary source for ACT UP formation, recruitment strategies, protest development, McCrery actions, and internal organizing in Shreveport.
9. **Gary Cathey—Oral history interviews (*Small Town Rage* project, 2012–2017; Interviews, September 2025; November 2025).** Source for ACT UP leadership, protest actions, and personal consequences of activism, particularly in Shreveport.
10. **ACT UP Oral History Project—Archival interviews and video materials (2001–present).** Participant testimony and documentation of national ACT UP actions, including the "Storm the NIH" demonstration and its implications for local movements like ACT UP Shreveport.
11. **Gary Cathey—Correspondence (early 1990s).** Letter to Jim McCrery addressing AIDS policy positions, rhetoric, and constituent impact.

12. **Freeman and Harris Café—Organizational and community space (1980s–1990s)**. Cultural hub for Black Shreveport, where political and social discussions intersected with activism, including early conversations around AIDS and community care.

13. The *Shreveport Journal*—Newspaper (**June 12, 1985**). Coverage of ACT UP response to early AIDS cases and growing public awareness.

14. *Bossier Press-Tribune*—Newspaper (**July 1987**). Coverage of AIDS education efforts and regional awareness campaigns within Bossier City.

15. **Louisiana Department of Health and Hospitals—State records (early 1990s)**. Documentation of the state's response to the AIDS crisis and distribution of care, including funding discrepancies and regional health policies.

16. **ACT UP Oral History Project—Video interviews and archival materials (2001–present)**. Includes participant testimony and firsthand accounts of the May 21, 1990 "Storm the NIH" demonstration.

17. The *Shreveport Times*—Newspaper (**January 1990**). Coverage of ACT UP's confrontation with workplace discrimination after Vern Ransburg Jr. was fired due to his HIV status.

18. The *Advocate*—Publication (**October 1990**). Coverage of ACT UP's public intervention during Shreveport's annual Holocaust Remembrance service.

19. **ACT UP Oral History Project—Video interviews and archival materials (2001–present)**. Includes interviews with participants in the AIDS Quilt's early displays in Shreveport and Bossier City.

20. **Louisiana State University Shreveport—Noel Memorial Library Special Collections (2012–present)**. Repository for ACT UP Shreveport materials including organizational documents, film footage, interviews, and research notes associated with the *Small Town Rage* project.

21. **Kurt Pickett—Personal writings and recorded materials (1980s–1991)**. Includes journals, published writings, and recollections preserved through interviews and family accounts.

22. **Chuck Selber—Writings, performances, and recorded media (1980s–1991)**. Includes theatrical work, public statements, and news footage; supplemented by ACT UP member oral histories.

23. **Joe DeSantis—Posthumous oral history** (*Small Town Rage* project, 2012–2017; Interviews, August 2025; September 2025). Source for activism, arrest, abuse, and artistic contributions.

24. **Mark Zeidman—Oral history interviews** (*Small Town Rage* project, 2012–2017; Interviews, September 2025). Source for family perspective on Chuck Selber, including growing up with "Uncle Chuck" and the family's insights on his activism and death.

25. **Phyllis Selber—Oral history interviews** (*Small Town Rage* project, 2012–2017; Interviews, September 2025). Source for family perspective on

     DR. DAVID W. HYLAN

Chuck Selber's upbringing, activism, and death, as well as the emotional and political impact of his life on the family. Also, source for words spoken to Flo Selber regarding Chuck Selber's death.

26. **Jill Selber Handaly—Oral history interviews (*Small Town Rage* project, 2012–2017; Interviews, August 2025).** Source for personal perspective on Chuck Selber's life and legacy, including growing up with "Uncle Chuck" and reflections on his activism.

27. **Kay Zeidman—Oral history interviews (*Small Town Rage* project, 2012–2017; Interviews, August 2025; November 2025).** Source for family perspective on Chuck Selber, including childhood memories, familial impressions, and recollections of his activism and personal life.

28. **Flo Selber—Correspondence and writings (1980s–1990s).** Includes letters to the editor, written contributions to public discourse, and reflections on her son Chuck Selber's activism and death. Also includes film interview for Small Town Rage.

29. **Robert Darrow—Oral history interviews (*Small Town Rage* project, 2012–2017; Interviews, September 2025; October 2025).** Source for ACT UP formation, actions, strategy, medical advocacy, HIV treatments, and local response to AIDS in Shreveport.

CHAPTER 4: LOCAL STRUGGLES

1. *Small Town Rage*—**Documentary film (2016).** Visual and narrative record confirming events, participant accounts, and protest actions of ACT UP Shreveport, including Chuck Selber's leadership and the group's local confrontations.

2. *Small Town Rage*—**Final transcript (2012–2016).** Primary oral-history backbone for verified quotations, speaker identification, and event reconstruction, particularly focusing on Chuck Selber, Gary Cathey, and other ACT UP members.

3. **ACT UP Shreveport—Organizational archive and protest documents (1989–1993).** Internal and public materials including memos, press releases, flyers, stickers, correspondence, and campaign messaging used to organize actions and communicate demands.

4. The *Advocate*—**Publication (September 1992).** Coverage of McCrery controversy and ACT UP response, highlighting public confrontation and media's role in shaping the crisis narrative.

5. The *Shreveport Times*—**Newspaper (September 2, 1983; September 14, 1985; 1992; August 1993; December 1993).** Coverage of AIDS cases, public response, funding disparities, and memorial reflections in Shreveport and surrounding areas.

6. Zinn Education Project—Publication (May 21, 1990). Overview of ACT UP's "Storm the NIH" action, framing the national movement and contextualizing regional responses like those in Shreveport.

7. Deborah Allen—Oral history interviews (*Small Town Rage* project, 2012–2017; Interviews, August 2025; November 2025; February 2026). Primary source for ACT UP formation, recruitment strategies, protest development, McCrery actions, and internal organizing in Shreveport.

8. Gary Cathey—Oral history interviews (*Small Town Rage* project, 2012–2017; Interviews, September 2025; November 2025). Source for ACT UP leadership, protest actions, and personal consequences of activism, particularly in Shreveport.

9. ACT UP Oral History Project—Archival interviews and video materials (2001–present). Participant testimony and documentation of national ACT UP actions, including the "Storm the NIH" demonstration and its implications for local movements like ACT UP Shreveport.

10. Robert Darrow—Oral history interviews (*Small Town Rage* project, 2012–2017; Interviews, September 2025; October 2025). Source for ACT UP actions and strategy process.

11. The *Shreveport Times*—newspaper coverage (1980s–1990s). Local reporting on HIV/AIDS education debates, including the promotion and controversy surrounding Sex Respect curricula.

12. Robert Darrow—"AIDS: Conservative roadblocks killing our children" (guest column, The *Shreveport Times*, May 30, 1992). Argues against abstinence-only education and calls for comprehensive HIV/AIDS prevention in Louisiana schools.

13. Robert Darrow—Oral history interviews (*Small Town Rage* project, 2012–2017; Interviews, September 2025; October 2025). Source for ACT UP formation, actions, strategy, medical advocacy, HIV treatments, and local response to AIDS in Shreveport.

14. Gary Cathey—Correspondence (early 1990s). Letter to Jim McCrery addressing AIDS policy positions, rhetoric, and constituent impact.

15. Freeman and Harris Café—Organizational and community space (1980s–1990s). Cultural hub for Black Shreveport, where political and social discussions intersected with activism, including early conversations around AIDS and community care.

16. The *Shreveport Journal*—Newspaper (June 12, 1985). Coverage of ACT UP response to early AIDS cases and growing public awareness.

17. *Bossier Press-Tribune*—Newspaper (July 1987). Coverage of AIDS education efforts and regional awareness campaigns within Bossier City.

18. Louisiana Department of Health and Hospitals—State records (early 1990s). Documentation of the state's response to the AIDS crisis and distribution of care, including funding discrepancies and regional health policies.

19. **ACT UP Oral History Project—Video interviews and archival materials (2001–present).** Includes participant testimony and firsthand accounts of the May 21, 1990 "Storm the NIH" demonstration.

20. **The *Shreveport Times*—Newspaper (January 1990).** Coverage of ACT UP's confrontation with workplace discrimination after Vern Ransburg Jr. was fired due to his HIV status.

21. **The *Advocate*—Publication (October 1990).** Coverage of ACT UP's public intervention during Shreveport's annual Holocaust Remembrance service.

22. **ACT UP Oral History Project—Video interviews and archival materials (2001–present).** Includes interviews with participants in the AIDS Quilt's early displays in Shreveport and Bossier City.

23. **Louisiana State University Shreveport—Noel Memorial Library Special Collections (2012–present).** Repository for ACT UP Shreveport materials including organizational documents, film footage, interviews, and research notes associated with the *Small Town Rage* project.

CHAPTER 5: STATE AND NATIONAL COLLABORATIONS

1. *Small Town Rage*—**Documentary film (2016).** Visual and narrative record confirming events, participant accounts, and protest actions of ACT UP Shreveport, including national collaboration and lobbying efforts.

2. *Small Town Rage*—**Final transcript (2012–2016).** Primary oral-history backbone for verified quotations, speaker identification, and event reconstruction, especially regarding Alana Oldham, Gary Cathey, and other ACT UP members.

3. **ACT UP Shreveport—Organizational archive and protest documents (1989–1993).** Internal and public materials including memos, press releases, flyers, stickers, correspondence, and campaign messaging used to organize actions and communicate demands.

4. **The *Advocate*—Publication (September 1992).** Coverage of McCrery controversy and ACT UP response, highlighting public confrontation and media's role in shaping the crisis narrative.

5. **The *Shreveport Times*—Newspaper (September 2, 1983; September 14, 1985; 1992; August 1993; December 1993).** Coverage of AIDS cases, public response, funding disparities, and memorial reflections in Shreveport and surrounding areas.

6. **Zinn Education Project—Publication (May 21, 1990).** Overview of ACT UP's "Storm the NIH" action, framing the national movement and contextualizing regional responses like those in Shreveport.

7. **Robert Darrow—Oral history interviews (*Small Town Rage* project, 2012–2017; Interviews, September 2025; October 2025).** Source for

ACT UP formation, actions, strategy, medical advocacy, HIV treatments, and local response to AIDS in Shreveport.

8. **Deborah Allen—Oral history interviews (*Small Town Rage* project, 2012–2017; Interviews, August 2025; November 2025; February 2026).** Primary source for ACT UP formation, recruitment strategies, protest development, McCrery actions, and internal organizing in Shreveport.

9. **Gary Cathey—Oral history interviews (*Small Town Rage* project, 2012–2017; Interviews, September 2025; November 2025).** Source for ACT UP leadership, protest actions, and personal consequences of activism, particularly in Shreveport.

10. **ACT UP Oral History Project—Archival interviews and video materials (2001–present).** Participant testimony and documentation of national ACT UP actions, including the "Storm the NIH" demonstration and its implications for local movements like ACT UP Shreveport.

11. **Gary Cathey—Correspondence (early 1990s).** Letter to Jim McCrery addressing AIDS policy positions, rhetoric, and constituent impact.

12. **Freeman and Harris Café—Organizational and community space (1980s–1990s).** Cultural hub for Black Shreveport, where political and social discussions intersected with activism, including early conversations around AIDS and community care.

13. **The *Shreveport Journal*—Newspaper (June 12, 1985).** Coverage of ACT UP response to early AIDS cases and growing public awareness.

14. ***Bossier Press-Tribune*—Newspaper (July 1987).** Coverage of AIDS education efforts and regional awareness campaigns within Bossier City.

15. **Louisiana Department of Health and Hospitals—State records (early 1990s).** Documentation of the state's response to the AIDS crisis and distribution of care, including funding discrepancies and regional health policies.

16. **ACT UP Oral History Project—Video interviews and archival materials (2001–present).** Includes participant testimony and firsthand accounts of the May 21, 1990 "Storm the NIH" demonstration.

17. **The *Shreveport Times*—Newspaper (January 1990).** Coverage of ACT UP's confrontation with workplace discrimination after Vern Ransburg Jr. was fired due to his HIV status.

18. **The *Advocate*—Publication (October 1990).** Coverage of ACT UP's public intervention during Shreveport's annual Holocaust Remembrance service.

19. **ACT UP Oral History Project—Video interviews and archival materials (2001–present).** Includes interviews with participants in the AIDS Quilt's early displays in Shreveport and Bossier City.

20. **Louisiana State University Shreveport—Noel Memorial Library Special Collections (2012–present).** Repository for ACT UP Shreveport materials including organizational documents, film footage, interviews, and research notes associated with the *Small Town Rage* project.

　　　　　　　　DR. DAVID W. HYLAN

<h1 style="text-align:center">CHAPTER 6: SILENCE AND EXPOSURE</h1>

1. *Small Town Rage*—Documentary film (2016). Visual and narrative record confirming events, participant accounts, and protest actions of ACT UP Shreveport, especially related to Jim McCrery's public denial and Gary Cathey's role in revealing the truth.

2. *Small Town Rage*—Final transcript (2012–2016). Primary oral-history backbone for verified quotations, speaker identification, and event reconstruction, focusing on Gary Cathey, Chuck Selber, Deborah Allen, and other ACT UP members.

3. ACT UP Shreveport—Organizational archive and protest documents (1989–1993). Internal and public materials including memos, press releases, flyers, stickers, correspondence, and campaign messaging used to organize actions and communicate demands.

4. The *Advocate*—Publication (September 1992). Coverage of McCrery controversy and ACT UP response, particularly focusing on the article "The Outing of a Family Values Congressman."

5. The *Shreveport Times*—Newspaper (September 2, 1983; September 14, 1985; 1992; August 1993; December 1993). Coverage of AIDS cases, public response, funding disparities, and memorial reflections in Shreveport and surrounding areas.

6. Zinn Education Project—Publication (May 21, 1990). Overview of ACT UP's "Storm the NIH" action, framing the national movement and contextualizing regional responses like those in Shreveport.

7. Deborah Allen—Oral history interviews (*Small Town Rage* project, 2012–2017; Interviews, August 2025; November 2025; February 2026). Primary source for ACT UP formation, recruitment strategies, protest development, McCrery actions, and internal organizing in Shreveport.

8. Gary Cathey—Oral history interviews (*Small Town Rage* project, 2012–2017; Interviews, September 2025; November 2025). Source for ACT UP leadership, protest actions, and personal consequences of activism, particularly in Shreveport.

9. ACT UP Oral History Project—Archival interviews and video materials (2001–present). Participant testimony and documentation of national ACT UP actions, including the "Storm the NIH" demonstration and its implications for local movements like ACT UP Shreveport.

10. Gary Cathey—Correspondence (early 1990s). Letter to Jim McCrery addressing AIDS policy positions, rhetoric, and constituent impact.

11. Freeman and Harris Café—Organizational and community space (1980s–1990s). Cultural hub for Black Shreveport, where political and social discussions intersected with activism, including early conversations around AIDS and community care.

12. The *Shreveport Journal*—Newspaper (June 12, 1985). Coverage of ACT UP response to early AIDS cases and growing public awareness.

13. *Bossier Press-Tribune*—Newspaper (July 1987). Coverage of AIDS education efforts and regional awareness campaigns within Bossier City.

14. **Louisiana Department of Health and Hospitals—State records (early 1990s).** Documentation of the state's response to the AIDS crisis and distribution of care, including funding discrepancies and regional health policies.

15. **ACT UP Oral History Project—Video interviews and archival materials (2001–present).** Includes participant testimony and firsthand accounts of the May 21, 1990 "Storm the NIH" demonstration.

16. The *Shreveport Times*—Newspaper (January 1990). Coverage of ACT UP's confrontation with workplace discrimination after Vern Ransburg Jr. was fired due to his HIV status.

17. The *Advocate*—Publication (October 1990). Coverage of ACT UP's public intervention during Shreveport's annual Holocaust Remembrance service.

18. **ACT UP Oral History Project—Video interviews and archival materials (2001–present).** Includes interviews with participants in the AIDS Quilt's early displays in Shreveport and Bossier City.

19. **Louisiana State University Shreveport—Noel Memorial Library Special Collections (2012–present).** Repository for ACT UP Shreveport materials including organizational documents, film footage, interviews, and research notes associated with the *Small Town Rage* project.

20. **Robert Darrow—Oral history interviews (*Small Town Rage* project, 2012-2017; Interviews, September 2025; October 2025).** Source for ACT UP formation, actions, strategy, medical advocacy, HIV treatments, and local response to AIDS in Shreveport, establishment of the Philadelphia Center.

CHAPTER 7: CAST OF RAGE

1. *Small Town Rage*—Documentary film (2016). Visual and narrative record confirming events, participant accounts, and protest actions of ACT UP Shreveport, including Chuck Selber's leadership and the group's local confrontations.

2. *Small Town Rage*—Final transcript (2012–2016). Primary oral-history backbone for verified quotations, speaker identification, and event reconstruction, particularly focusing on Chuck Selber, Gary Cathey, and other ACT UP members.

3. **ACT UP Shreveport—Organizational archive and protest documents (1989–1993).** Internal and public materials including memos, press releases, flyers, stickers, correspondence, and campaign messaging used to organize actions and communicate demands.

　　　　　DR. DAVID W. HYLAN

4. The *Advocate*—Publication (September 1992). Coverage of McCrery controversy and ACT UP response, highlighting public confrontation and media's role in shaping the crisis narrative.

5. The *Shreveport Times*—Newspaper (September 2, 1983; September 14, 1985; 1992; August 1993; December 1993). Coverage of AIDS cases, public response, funding disparities, and memorial reflections in Shreveport and surrounding areas.

6. Zinn Education Project—Publication (May 21, 1990). Overview of ACT UP's "Storm the NIH" action, framing the national movement and contextualizing regional responses like those in Shreveport.

7. Deborah Allen—Oral history interviews (*Small Town Rage* project, 2012–2017; Interviews, August 2025; November 2025; February 2026). Primary source for ACT UP formation, recruitment strategies, protest development, McCrery actions, and internal organizing in Shreveport.

8. Gary Cathey—Oral history interviews (*Small Town Rage* project, 2012–2017; Interviews, September 2025; November 2025). Source for ACT UP leadership, protest actions, and personal consequences of activism, particularly in Shreveport.

9. ACT UP Oral History Project—Archival interviews and video materials (2001–present). Participant testimony and documentation of national ACT UP actions, including the "Storm the NIH" demonstration and its implications for local movements like ACT UP Shreveport.

10. Gary Cathey—Correspondence (early 1990s). Letter to Jim McCrery addressing AIDS policy positions, rhetoric, and constituent impact.

11. Freeman and Harris Café—Organizational and community space (1980s–1990s). Cultural hub for Black Shreveport, where political and social discussions intersected with activism, including early conversations around AIDS and community care.

12. The *Shreveport Journal*—Newspaper (June 12, 1985). Coverage of ACT UP response to early AIDS cases and growing public awareness.

13. *Bossier Press-Tribune*—Newspaper (July 1987). Coverage of AIDS education efforts and regional awareness campaigns within Bossier City.

14. Louisiana Department of Health and Hospitals—State records (early 1990s). Documentation of the state's response to the AIDS crisis and distribution of care, including funding discrepancies and regional health policies.

15. ACT UP Oral History Project—Video interviews and archival materials (2001–present). Includes participant testimony and firsthand accounts of the May 21, 1990 "Storm the NIH" demonstration.

16. The *Shreveport Times*—Newspaper (January 1990). Coverage of ACT UP's confrontation with workplace discrimination after Vern Ransburg Jr. was fired due to his HIV status.

17. The *Advocate*—Publication (October 1990). Coverage of ACT UP's public intervention during Shreveport's annual Holocaust Remembrance service.
18. **ACT UP Oral History Project—Video interviews and archival materials (2001–present).** Includes interviews with participants in the AIDS Quilt's early displays in Shreveport and Bossier City.
19. **Louisiana State University Shreveport—Noel Memorial Library Special Collections (2012–present).** Repository for ACT UP Shreveport materials including organizational documents, film footage, interviews, and research notes associated with the *Small Town Rage* project.
20. **Kurt Pickett—Personal writings and recorded materials (1980s–1991).** Includes journals, published writings, and recollections preserved through interviews and family accounts.
21. **Chuck Selber—Writings, performances, and recorded media (1980s–1991).** Includes theatrical work, public statements, and news footage; supplemented by ACT UP member oral histories.
22. **Joe DeSantis—Posthumous oral history (*Small Town Rage* project, 2012–2017; Interviews, August 2025; September 2025).** Source for activism, arrest, abuse, and artistic contributions.
23. **Marcus Spurlock—Oral history interviews (*Small Town Rage* project, 2012–2017).** Source for medical and activist connections, as well as participation in early ACT UP strategy meetings. c
24. **Robert Darrow—Oral history interviews (*Small Town Rage* project, 2012–2017; Interviews, September 2025; October 2025).** Source for ACT UP formation, actions, strategy, medical advocacy, HIV treatments, and local response to AIDS in Shreveport.

CHAPTER 8: THE PHILADELPHIA CENTER

1. *Small Town Rage*—**Documentary film (2016).** Visual and narrative record confirming events, participant accounts, and protest actions of ACT UP Shreveport, including the role of the Philadelphia Center in the ongoing fight for care and dignity.
2. *Small Town Rage*—**Final transcript (2012–2016).** Primary oral-history backbone for verified quotations, speaker identification, and event reconstruction, with insights from Marcus Spurlock, Robert Darrow, Gary Cathey, and others who helped establish the Philadelphia Center.
3. **ACT UP Shreveport—Organizational archive and protest documents (1989–1993).** Internal and public materials including memos, press releases, flyers, stickers, correspondence, and campaign messaging used to organize actions and communicate demands, including advocacy for healthcare reform and the establishment of local services.

4. The *Advocate*—Publication (**September 1992**). Coverage of McCrery controversy and ACT UP response, focusing on the public confrontation and the media's role in pushing for AIDS awareness in the region.

5. The *Shreveport Times*—Newspaper (**September 2, 1983; September 14, 1985; 1992; August 1993; December 1993**). Coverage of AIDS cases, public response, funding disparities, and memorial reflections in Shreveport, highlighting the local struggles of the HIV/AIDS epidemic.

6. **Zinn Education Project**—Publication (**May 21, 1990**). Overview of ACT UP's "Storm the NIH" action, framing the national movement and contextualizing the local response in Shreveport.

7. **Deborah Allen**—Oral history interviews (*Small Town Rage* project, **2012–2017; Interviews, August 2025; November 2025; February 2026**). Primary source for ACT UP formation, recruitment strategies, protest development, McCrery actions, and internal organizing in Shreveport, including connections to the Philadelphia Center's creation.

8. **Gary Cathey**—Oral history interviews (*Small Town Rage* project, **2012–2017; Interviews, September 2025; November 2025**). Source for ACT UP leadership, protest actions, and personal consequences of activism, including his role in the advocacy for the Philadelphia Center.

9. **ACT UP Oral History Project**—Archival interviews and video materials (**2001–present**). Participant testimony and documentation of national ACT UP actions, including the "Storm the NIH" demonstration and the implications for local movements like ACT UP Shreveport and the Philadelphia Center.

10. **Gary Cathey**—Correspondence (**early 1990s**). Letter to Jim McCrery addressing AIDS policy positions, rhetoric, and constituent impact, including advocacy for local AIDS services.

11. **Freeman and Harris Café**—Organizational and community space (**1980s–1990s**). Cultural hub for Black Shreveport, where political and social discussions intersected with activism, including early conversations about AIDS and the need for community-based care.

12. The *Shreveport Journal*—Newspaper (**June 12, 1985**). Coverage of ACT UP response to early AIDS cases and the growing public awareness of the epidemic.

13. *Bossier Press-Tribune*—Newspaper (**July 1987**). Coverage of AIDS education efforts and regional awareness campaigns within Bossier City, aligning with ACT UP's broader mission.

14. **Louisiana Department of Health and Hospitals**—State records (**early 1990s**). Documentation of the state's response to the AIDS crisis, including funding discrepancies, healthcare distribution, and the regional challenges addressed by ACT UP and the Philadelphia Center.

15. **ACT UP Oral History Project**—Video interviews and archival materials

(2001–present). Includes participant testimony and firsthand accounts of the May 21, 1990 "Storm the NIH" demonstration and other pivotal actions that helped lay the foundation for the Philadelphia Center.

16. The *Shreveport Times*—Newspaper (**January 1990**). Coverage of ACT UP's confrontation with workplace discrimination and the early push for local healthcare reform for HIV-positive individuals.

17. The *Advocate*—**Publication (October 1990)**. Coverage of ACT UP's public intervention during Shreveport's annual Holocaust Remembrance service and its connections to AIDS activism.

18. **ACT UP Oral History Project—Video interviews and archival materials (2001–present).** Includes interviews with participants involved in organizing for the Philadelphia Center and AIDS awareness in Shreveport.

19. **Louisiana State University Shreveport—Noel Memorial Library Special Collections (2012–present).** Repository for ACT UP Shreveport materials, including organizational documents, film footage, interviews, and research notes related to the development of the Philadelphia Center.

20. **Robert Darrow—Oral history interviews (*Small Town Rage* project, 2012-2017; Interviews, September 2025; October 2025).** Source for ACT UP formation, actions, strategy, medical advocacy, HIV treatments, and local response to AIDS in Shreveport, establishment of the Philadelphia Center.

CHAPTER 9: THE MAKING OF *SMALL TOWN RAGE*

1. *Small Town Rage*—**Documentary film (2016).** Visual and narrative record confirming events, participant accounts, and protest actions of ACT UP Shreveport, including the creation and impact of the film.

2. *Small Town Rage*—**Final transcript (2012–2016).** Primary oral-history backbone for verified quotations, speaker identification, and event reconstruction, particularly focusing on the experiences of Raydra Hall, Gary Cathey, and other key contributors to the film.

3. **ACT UP Shreveport—Organizational archive and protest documents (1989–1993).** Internal and public materials including memos, press releases, flyers, stickers, correspondence, and campaign messaging used to organize actions and communicate demands, setting the stage for the film's exploration.

4. The *Advocate*—**Publication (September 1992).** Coverage of McCrery controversy and ACT UP response, particularly focusing on the public confrontation and media's role in shaping the crisis narrative.

5. The *Shreveport Times*—**Newspaper (September 2, 1983; September 14, 1985; 1992; August 1993; December 1993).** Coverage of AIDS cases, public response, funding disparities, and memorial reflections in Shreveport and surrounding areas.

6. **Zinn Education Project—Publication (May 21, 1990).** Overview of ACT UP's "Storm the NIH" action, framing the national movement and contextualizing regional responses like those in Shreveport.

7. **Deborah Allen—Oral history interviews (*Small Town Rage* project, 2012–2017; Interviews, August 2025; November 2025; February 2026).** Primary source for ACT UP formation, recruitment strategies, protest development, McCrery actions, and internal organizing in Shreveport, including her perspective on the making of the film.

8. **Gary Cathey—Oral history interviews (*Small Town Rage* project, 2012–2017; Interviews, September 2025; November 2025).** Source for ACT UP leadership, protest actions, and personal consequences of activism, particularly in Shreveport, including reflections on the film's creation.

9. **ACT UP Oral History Project—Archival interviews and video materials (2001–present).** Participant testimony and documentation of national ACT UP actions, including the "Storm the NIH" demonstration and its implications for local movements like ACT UP Shreveport.

10. **Gary Cathey—Correspondence (early 1990s).** Letter to Jim McCrery addressing AIDS policy positions, rhetoric, and constituent impact.

11. **Freeman and Harris Café—Organizational and community space (1980s–1990s).** Cultural hub for Black Shreveport, where political and social discussions intersected with activism, including early conversations around AIDS and the need for community-based care.

12. **The *Shreveport Journal*—Newspaper (June 12, 1985).** Coverage of ACT UP response to early AIDS cases and growing public awareness.

13. ***Bossier Press-Tribune*—Newspaper (July 1987).** Coverage of AIDS education efforts and regional awareness campaigns within Bossier City.

14. **Louisiana Department of Health and Hospitals—State records (early 1990s).** Documentation of the state's response to the AIDS crisis and distribution of care, including funding discrepancies and regional health policies.

15. **ACT UP Oral History Project—Video interviews and archival materials (2001–present).** Includes participant testimony and firsthand accounts of the May 21, 1990 "Storm the NIH" demonstration.

16. **The *Shreveport Times*—Newspaper (January 1990).** Coverage of ACT UP's confrontation with workplace discrimination after Vern Ransburg Jr. was fired due to his HIV status.

17. **The *Advocate*—Publication (October 1990).** Coverage of ACT UP's public intervention during Shreveport's annual Holocaust Remembrance service.

18. **ACT UP Oral History Project—Video interviews and archival materials (2001–present).** Includes interviews with participants in the AIDS Quilt's early displays in Shreveport and Bossier City.

19. **Louisiana State University Shreveport—Noel Memorial Library Special**

Collections (2012–present). Repository for ACT UP Shreveport materials including organizational documents, film footage, interviews, and research notes associated with the *Small Town Rage* project.

20. **Kurt Pickett—Personal writings and recorded materials (1980s–1991).** Includes journals, published writings, and recollections preserved through interviews and family accounts.

21. **Chuck Selber—Writings, performances, and recorded media (1980s–1991).** Includes theatrical work, public statements, and news footage; supplemented by ACT UP member oral histories.

22. **Joe DeSantis—Posthumous oral history (*Small Town Rage* project, 2012–2017; Interviews, August 2025; September 2025).** Source for activism, arrest, abuse, and artistic contributions.

23. **Marcus Spurlock—Oral history interviews (*Small Town Rage* project, 2012–2017).** Source for medical and activist connections, as well as participation in early ACT UP strategy meetings.

24. **Robert Darrow—Oral history interviews (*Small Town Rage* project, 2012–2017; Interviews, September 2025; October 2025).** Source for medical advocacy, HIV treatments, and local response to AIDS in Shreveport.

25. **Clint McCommon—Oral history interviews (*Small Town Rage* project, 2012–2017; Interviews, August 2025).** Source for film production work, including technical and logistical contributions.

26. **John Chambers—Oral history interviews (*Small Town Rage* project, 2012–2017; Interviews, September 2025).** Source for film editing, production decisions, and collaboration with the filmmakers.

27. **Mollie Corbit—Photography and Kickstarter campaign material (2015).** Photographer and coordinator for the Kickstarter campaign video, contributing to the visual identity and outreach for the project.

28. **Anton Winder—Interactive media development (2016).** Developed an interactive touchscreen program for the *Small Town Rage* project, facilitating thematic exploration of raw footage.

29. **Gregory Kallenberg—Oral history interviews (*Small Town Rage* project, 2012–2017).** Source for advice on filmmaking process and involvement with the project, particularly in early stages.

30. **Clint McCommon and John Chambers—Documentary collaborators (*Small Town Rage* project, 2012–2017).** Collaborative filmmakers providing editing and production expertise, integral to the completion of the film.

31. **Lance Bass—Narrator, voiceover work (2016).** Source for the narration of *Small Town Rage*, lending his voice to the project after extensive discussions and collaboration with the filmmakers.

32. **Broadway Cares/Equity Fights AIDS—Sponsorship and funding (2015–2016).** Source of funding for the film's production, contributing critical support to the documentary's completion and festival screenings.

      DR. DAVID W. HYLAN

33. **Film Prize Foundation—Festival sponsorship (2015–2016).** Partnered with *Small Town Rage* for festival screenings, supporting the film's recognition and public engagement in Louisiana.

34. **Film Prize Festival—Screening and award (2015).** Host of the Louisiana premiere for *Small Town Rage*, providing a platform for the film to be shown and recognized in the public sphere.

35. **Robert Darrow—Oral history interviews (*Small Town Rage* project, 2012-2017; Interviews, September 2025; October 2025).** Source for ACT UP formation, actions, strategy, medical advocacy, HIV treatments, and local response to AIDS in Shreveport, establishment of the Philadelphia Center.

CHAPTER 10: LEGACY AND AFTERMATH

1. *Small Town Rage*—Documentary film (2016). Visual and narrative record confirming events, participant accounts, and protest actions of ACT UP Shreveport, including the legacy of the movement and the creation of the Philadelphia Center.

2. *Small Town Rage*—Final transcript (2012–2016). Primary oral-history backbone for verified quotations, speaker identification, and event reconstruction, particularly focusing on the reflections of Deborah Allen, Gary Cathey, Kenny King, and others involved in the film and legacy.

3. **ACT UP Shreveport—Organizational archive and protest documents (1989–1993).** Internal and public materials including memos, press releases, flyers, stickers, correspondence, and campaign messaging used to organize actions and communicate demands, setting the stage for the film's exploration and impact.

4. The *Advocate*—Publication (September 1992). Coverage of McCrery controversy and ACT UP response, particularly focusing on the public confrontation and the media's role in shaping the crisis narrative.

5. The *Shreveport Times*—Newspaper (September 2, 1983; September 14, 1985; 1992; August 1993; December 1993). Coverage of AIDS cases, public response, funding disparities, and memorial reflections in Shreveport and surrounding areas, setting the stage for ACT UP's public battle for dignity.

6. **Zinn Education Project—Publication (May 21, 1990).** Overview of ACT UP's "Storm the NIH" action, framing the national movement and contextualizing regional responses like those in Shreveport.

7. **Deborah Allen—Oral history interviews (*Small Town Rage* project, 2012–2017; Interviews, August 2025; November 2025; February 2026).** Primary source for ACT UP formation, recruitment strategies, protest development, McCrery actions, and internal organizing in Shreveport,

including reflections on the shift from activism to institutional work with the Philadelphia Center.

8. **Gary Cathey—Oral history interviews (*Small Town Rage* project, 2012–2017; Interviews, September 2025; November 2025).** Source for ACT UP leadership, protest actions, personal consequences of activism, and the legacy of the movement, particularly in the context of the Philadelphia Center's formation.

9. **ACT UP Oral History Project—Archival interviews and video materials (2001–present).** Participant testimony and documentation of national ACT UP actions, including the "Storm the NIH" demonstration and its implications for local movements like ACT UP Shreveport.

10. **Gary Cathey—Correspondence (early 1990s).** Letter to Jim McCrery addressing AIDS policy positions, rhetoric, and constituent impact, underscoring the national and local dimensions of ACT UP's activism.

11. **Freeman and Harris Café—Organizational and community space (1980s–1990s).** Cultural hub for Black Shreveport, where political and social discussions intersected with activism, including early conversations around AIDS and community care.

12. **The *Shreveport Journal*—Newspaper (June 12, 1985).** Coverage of ACT UP response to early AIDS cases and growing public awareness.

13. ***Bossier Press-Tribune*—Newspaper (July 1987).** Coverage of AIDS education efforts and regional awareness campaigns within Bossier City, aligning with ACT UP's broader mission.

14. **Louisiana Department of Health and Hospitals—State records (early 1990s).** Documentation of the state's response to the AIDS crisis and distribution of care, including funding discrepancies and regional health policies.

15. **ACT UP Oral History Project—Video interviews and archival materials (2001–present).** Includes participant testimony and firsthand accounts of the May 21, 1990 "Storm the NIH" demonstration and its broader impact.

16. **The *Shreveport Times*—Newspaper (January 1990).** Coverage of ACT UP's confrontation with workplace discrimination after Vern Ransburg Jr. was fired due to his HIV status.

17. **The *Advocate*—Publication (October 1990).** Coverage of ACT UP's public intervention during Shreveport's annual Holocaust Remembrance service and its connections to AIDS activism.

18. **ACT UP Oral History Project—Video interviews and archival materials (2001–present).** Includes interviews with participants involved in organizing for the Philadelphia Center and AIDS awareness in Shreveport.

19. **Louisiana State University Shreveport—Noel Memorial Library Special Collections (2012–present).** Repository for ACT UP Shreveport materials, including organizational documents, film footage, interviews, and research notes associated with the *Small Town Rage* project.

20. **Kurt Pickett—Personal writings and recorded materials (1980s–1991).** Includes journals, published writings, and recollections preserved through interviews and family accounts.
21. **Chuck Selber—Writings, performances, and recorded media (1980s–1991).** Includes theatrical work, public statements, and news footage; supplemented by ACT UP member oral histories.
22. **Joe DeSantis—Posthumous oral history (*Small Town Rage* project, 2012–2017; Interviews, August 2025; September 2025).** Source for activism, arrest, abuse, and artistic contributions.
23. **Marcus Spurlock—Oral history interviews (*Small Town Rage* project, 2012–2017).** Source for medical and activist connections, as well as participation in early ACT UP strategy meetings.
24. **Robert Darrow—Oral history interviews (*Small Town Rage* project, 2012–2017; Interviews, September 2025; October 2025).** Source for ACT UP formation, actions, strategy, medical advocacy, HIV treatments, and local response to AIDS in Shreveport.

BIBLIOGRAPHY

The *Advocate.* Coverage of ACT UP activism and Louisiana AIDS advocacy. September 1992.

The *Shreveport Times.* Coverage of AIDS cases, public response, activism, and memorialization in northwest Louisiana. 1983–2014.

The *Shreveport Journal.* Coverage of early AIDS awareness, local attitudes, and ACT UP activity in Shreveport. 1985–1990.

Bossier Press-Tribune. Coverage of regional AIDS education efforts and public awareness in Bossier City. 1987.

Darrow, Robert (Bobby). Letters to the editor and guest columns addressing HIV/AIDS policy, stigma, and public response. *The Shreveport Times* and *The Shreveport Journal*, 1991–1998.

Cathey, Gary. Letter to Congressman Jim McCrery encouraging him to live openly and authentically. Personal correspondence, 1992.

Hylan, David W., and Raydra Hall, directors. *Small Town Rage: Fighting Back in the Deep South.* Independent documentary film, 2017.

Schwartz, Malkie. "Chuck Selber's Purposeful Anger." *My Jewish Learning,* December 2013.

Small Town Rage—**Final Transcript.** Documentary transcript prepared for the film and companion book project.

ABOUT THE AUTHOR

Dr. David W. Hylan is a writer, filmmaker, and advocate whose work has long centered on voices pushed to the margins. He co-directed and co-produced the award-winning documentary *Small Town Rage: Fighting Back in the Deep South*, capturing the courage and confrontation of ACT UP Shreveport during one of the most turbulent chapters in American public health.

Raised in Shreveport, Louisiana, Hylan witnessed firsthand the silence, stigma, and resistance that defined the early years of the AIDS crisis in the Deep South. Decades later, that history became the foundation for this book.

For more than thirty-five years, he served as Executive Director of the Betty and Leonard Phillips Deaf Action Center, building programs rooted in access, dignity, and equity. He is also a co-founder of People Acting for Change and Equality (PACE), an LGBTQ+ advocacy organization in Northwest Louisiana that helped advance nondiscrimination protections in the region.

Hylan holds a doctorate in Leadership Studies from Louisiana State University, with a focus on nonprofit administration, and lives in Cozumel, Mexico, with his husband, Troy. *Small Town Rage: Fighting Back in the Deep South* is his first book.